Setting the *PACE*®
in Product Development
Revised Edition

Setting the *PACE*® in Product Development
Revised Edition

A Guide to *P*roduct *A*nd *C*ycle-time *E*xcellence®

Michael E. McGrath

EDITOR

Butterworth-Heinemann

Boston   Oxford   Johannesburg   Melbourne   New Delhi   Singapore

The following are registered trademarks of their respective holders: 3M, Ampex, Apollo, Apple Computer, AS/400, AS/6000, AT&T, ATM, AutoCAD, AutoCAD LT, AutoDesk, Band-Aid, Bolt, Beranek and Newman, Carrier Corporation, CAT Scanner, Codex, Conner Peripherals, CyberSURFER, Dataman, Digital Alpha/Windows NT, Digital Equipment Corporation, DuPont, Eastman Kodak, EMC Corporation, EMI, Excel, Fuji Xerox, GE, Hewlett Packard, IBM OS/2, IBM PC, Intel/Windows, JVC, Lotus Notes, Lotus Software, Mac, Macintosh, Macintosh Classic, Macintosh Classic II, Macintosh II, Macintosh Iifx, Macintosh Iix, Macintosh Lisa, Macintosh Plus, Macintosh SE, Matsushita, Microsoft, Motorola, Motorola 68000, MS-DOS, PowerBook, PowerBook 100, PowerBook 140, PowerBook 170, Quadra, RCA, Sony, Speak and Spell, Sun 2, Sun 3, Sun Microsystems, SunOS, Swatch, Swatch Twinphone, Tandem, Technicon, Texas Instruments, The Little Professor, Thomson Consumer Electronics, TI, Toshiba, UNIX, VAX, Windows 3.0, Xerox 5100, Xerox Corporation.

Library of Congress Cataloging-in-Publication Data
Setting the PACE in product development : a guide to product and cycle-
   time excellence / Michael E. McGrath, editor. -- Rev. ed.
      p.   cm.
   Rev. ed. of : Product development / Michael E. McGrath, Michael T.
Anthony, Amram R. Shapiro. c1992.
   Includes index.
   ISBN 0-7506-9789-X (pbk. : alk. paper)
   1. Production engineering. 2. New products. 3. Production
planning. I. McGrath, Michael E. II. McGrath, Michael E. Product
development.
TS176.S457   1996
658.5--dc20   96-12153
                                                       CIP

British Library Cataloguing-in-Publication Data
A catalogue record for this book is available from the British Library.

The publisher offers special discounts on bulk orders of this book.
For information, please contact:
Manager of Special Sales
Butterworth–Heinemann
313 Washington Street
Newton, MA 02158–1626
Tel: 617-928-2500
Fax: 617-928-2620

For information on all Business Books available, contact our World Wide Web home page at: http://www.bh.com

10 9 8

Printed in the United States of America

*We dedicate this book to the clients of
Pittiglio Rabin Todd & McGrath
— past, present, and future*

Table of Contents

6. Design Techniques and Automated Development Tools   85

Preface

Pittiglio Rabin Todd & McGrath (PRTM) initially developed the *Product And Cycle-time Excellence*®(PACE®)[1] product development process in 1986. Mike Anthony, Amram Shapiro, and I published the initial version of this book in 1992 to describe PACE. Since then, many companies have used it as the best-practice model for improving their product development processes. This new version of the book updates the best practices in PACE by incorporating new insights gained over several years.

In many ways PACE has become the de facto standard process reference model for product development. It provides a common framework, standard terminology, industry-wide process benchmarks, a way of updating best practices, and a process for continuous improvement.

Numerous companies have implemented PACE concepts, and PRTM has assisted more than 140 of them in their implementation. In fact, of the approximately $100 billion invested in R&D (research and development) by American companies in 1995, those using PACE account for more than $15 billion, or 15% of the total. This number is increasing as more and more companies are applying PACE to improve product development. When PACE originated back in 1986, American and European companies were trying to catch up to Japanese companies that had achieved a competitive advantage by implementing new manufacturing processes based on just-in-time (JIT) principles. We decided to identify the next operational process improvement that had the potential to change the competitive balance of industries. It was product development.

At that time most companies didn't even recognize product development as a process, but they were acutely aware of the need to improve the way they did product development. No company was satisfied with its development effectiveness. Also at that time, there were no standard process reference models for a highly effective product development process. So we developed, tested, and refined PACE.

All of the concepts, techniques, and management practices contained in PACE are not necessarily new or unique. Over the last five to ten years, many people have been trying to solve the problems associated with product development. Leading academics, such as Steve Wheelwright and Kim Clark at Harvard and Steve Rosenthal at Boston University, have done and continue to do some excellent research and writing in this area. Associations such as the PDMA (Product Development & Management Association) conduct research and conferences to promote the improvement of product development. Likewise, many very capable people in industry have advanced some of the management practices over the last five years.

There are two unique aspects of PACE. First, the PACE concepts, techniques, and management practices have subtle differences that make them more practicable and successful in actual implementation. Readers are encouraged to read each chapter carefully and not jump hastily to the conclusion that it must be exactly the same as something similar. Secondly, PACE is a complete framework. The individual elements, including the subtleties, work together to create a successful approach to improving product development.

This book, as was also the case with the earlier version, differs from the many other excellent books on product development in that it is empirically based rather than theoretically based. On any given day, PRTM is working with 20 to 25 major companies, helping them implement PACE. This extensive practical experience is generalized in PACE's best practices, and provides a practical complement to the excellent theoretical research done by others.

PACE's rapid acceptance has been fueled by the dramatic benefits that companies have achieved. We have found the following benefits to be typical:

- Time-to-market improvements of 40% to 60%
- Wasted product development reductions of 50% to 80%
- Product development productivity increases of 25% to 30%
- New product revenue (as a percentage of all revenue) increases of as much as 100%

These benefits are generally achieved by implementing the PACE project management elements: phase reviews, Core Teams, structured development, and development tools and techniques. These elements are essential to fast, high-quality, predictable project execution and constitute the first major stage of improvement. Our additional experience in implementing these has further validated the effectiveness of the original concepts. They work. Accordingly, we have made only minor modifications to the chapters (Chapters 3–6) that describe them, but we have added some thoughts in each of these chapters on where companies tend to go wrong.

Having successfully implemented the PACE project management elements and achieved the benefits described, companies then need to focus on the elements of cross-project management: product strategy, pipeline management, and technology management. We define these as the second major stage of improvement. The chapters (Chapters 7–9) describing these three elements have been completely rewritten to reflect rapidly evolving thought in this area.

The benefits derived from the cross-project management elements are less quantitative but more strategic. Managing product strategy as a process enables faster, more profitable growth. Pipeline management helps companies to deploy and balance resources to support multiple strategies. Technology management transforms technology development into an enabler for executing product strategies and achieving rapid, predictable time-to-market.

In Chapter 10, we describe the stages that companies typically go through in improving their product development processes. This framework helps companies position themselves along the stages of improvement and enables them to set targets for further improvement.

This updated version contains contributions from many people beyond Mike, Amram, and myself, reflecting the breadth and depth of PRTM's PACE consulting experience. For that reason there are more authors in this version. Each chapter identifies the author or authors of that chapter.

Many hundreds of man-years of consulting by PRTM consultants have continually enhanced the PACE methodologies, and it is impossible to acknowledge them all by name. Of special note, however, I would like to remember the contributions of Ted Pittiglio, one of PRTM's founders, to the development of PACE during its critical growing years. Ted passed away in 1994, but his contributions continue.

In completing this updated version we again have many people to thank. In particular, I would like to acknowledge the contributions of our world-class support staff, especially Beth Reed, who patiently pulled together the pieces of this book from many people.

Most of all, we would like to express our appreciation to the firm's clients. The challenges we tackle together with them continue to inspire us to push the state of the art farther and farther.

Michael E. McGrath
Pittiglio Rabin Todd & McGrath
Weston, Massachusetts
January 1996

---

1. PACE® and Product And Cycle-time Excellence® are registered service marks of Pittiglio Rabin Todd & McGrath.

CHAPTER 1

The Dramatic Change Taking Place in Product Development

Michael E. McGrath

In the first edition, published in 1992, we declared that product development would be the industrial battleground of the 1990s and into the next century, just as manufacturing was the industrial battleground of the 1970s and 1980s. Not only has this happened, but the impact is even greater than we had imagined.

The advantages that come from cutting time-to-market in half and consistently developing better products are so significant that the competitive balance in some industries is changing in favor of companies that can achieve these goals first. Companies introducing more new products, reacting faster to market and technology changes, and developing superior products are winning the battle over competitors.

There are many similarities between the change that took place in manufacturing in previous decades and the change taking place in product development today. Each is significant enough to achieve a real competitive advantage and is sustainable through continual improvement. In each case, the opportunity stems from redefining the underlying process using new management concepts.

The benefits attained by improving product development can be strategically significant, including increased revenue, improved development productivity, and operational efficiencies. Understanding the expected benefits establishes the performance levels that companies should expect from improving their product development processes. This is important because some companies mistakenly think that they have already made sufficient changes to

1

their product development processes, even though they have not seen a significant performance improvement.

Benefits of a More Effective Product Development Process

For most companies, improving the product development process will have a greater strategic impact than any other improvement they can make. They will grow faster. They will react to opportunities and threats faster than their competitors. They will significantly improve product development productivity and increase efficiencies in other operational areas as well.

Faster time-to-market is the most visible improvement, but as time-to-market improves, many other benefits result. And time-to-market has been steadily improving.

A 1995 benchmarking study on product development showed an average improvement in time-to-market of almost 10% from 1992 to 1994.[1] However, this average improvement was not the result of every company improving by 10%; it came from a small percentage of companies making significant improvements while the rest made little or none. As can be seen in Figure 1–1, the best-in-class companies (top 20%) had a time-to-market of 50% or less of the other companies in their industry. While this difference varies a little by

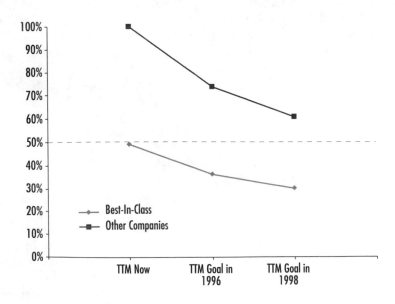

FIGURE 1–1 Comparative improvement in time-to-market (TTM) in technology-based companies.

industry, it was almost 50% in all technology-based industries. Figure 1–1 also shows the trend expected. While other companies expect to improve time-to-market by 40% by 1998, they will still not be where the best-in-class companies are today, and the best-in-class will continue to get even better.

In our experience, most companies can cut time-to-market in half with a better product development process. For example, the Codex division of Motorola cut its average product development time by 46% over a two-year period.[2] Similarly, Bolt, Beranek and Newman dramatically reduced time-to-market by 50%–60% for the first product developed with its new process.[3]

Increased Revenue

In most companies, significant improvements in time-to-market can fuel revenue growth, at least until competitors catch up by improving their own product development processes. Alternatively, if competitors are able to improve their product development process first, a company may see a decline in revenue.

Figure 1–2 clearly illustrates this difference in electronic systems companies.[4] The best-in-class companies have a much higher concentration of new products. Two years out, 75.3% of their revenue comes from new products, compared to a median of 44.7%. An increased level of new products usually

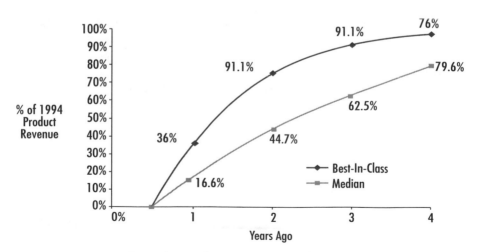

Note: New products are those introduced in the past 2 years

FIGURE 1–2   New product revenue as a percentage of total revenue in electronic systems companies.

In some volume-sensitive industries, the competitor who captures significant market share first is likely to be the low-cost producer. Costs continue to decline with experience, and second-tier competitors can never be as profitable.

Being first to market, however, does not always guarantee success. EMI developed the original CAT scanner but did not have the support and service necessary to be successful. Competitors such as GE and Technicon offered better service and support and were capable of developing a successful product. In 1979 EMI received the Nobel prize for the CAT scanner, but the company had to be acquired in order to be saved.

Success in time-sensitive markets

In some industries, the windows of market opportunity remain open for only a short time. In these cases, the ability to make any sales at all depends on time-to-market. Customer-specific components such as custom semiconductor devices fall into this category. If a company can develop the component in time for it to be designed into the customer's end product, then the company may be able to get that customer's business; if it can't, a competitor gets it. Time-to-market and predictability become sources of significant competitive advantage in industries such as these.

The computer workstation market is an example of a time-sensitive market. Most workstations are purchased by systems integrators, companies that integrate their own proprietary equipment and applications software into a system that they sell to specific users. While the life cycle of a new generation of workstations may be three to four years, the systems integrator selects the workstation around which it will build its system very quickly after the release of a new generation.

Sun Microsystems believes that it has only a year to convince customers to buy its new products. If customers select Sun in that first year, they are likely to continue to order products for another three or four years. If Sun is late by a year, however, the company feels it has missed the market. At the end of 1985, Sun introduced the Sun 3 product line to replace the Sun 2 product line introduced in 1983. The Sun 3 was developed in approximately one year, giving Sun a significant advantage. Because it came to market sooner, more systems integrators selected it as the basis for their systems. Sun Microsystems' revenue skyrocketed from $115 million in 1985 to more than $1 billion in three years. Sun's market share also leaped from 16% to 28%, while that of its major competitor, Apollo, dropped from 51% to 31%.

More successful products

Our experience in improving product development processes has also shown dramatic improvement in the success of new products. This stems from some of the aspects of a better process, such as the synergy of having people work more closely together, the design improvements of a more methodical process,

and the impact of better decision making. Marketing and engineering, for example, can make better trade-offs and find new opportunities. When this is
combined with the discipline of a more structured process, it helps to define
the right characteristics for the product.

Sometimes overlooked as a benefit is how shorter time-to-market provides an advantage in defining product requirements. The opportunity and requirements for a new product are defined at the beginning of a product
development project, but the market can change during the time it takes to develop the product. Customers may become interested in different features.
Prices may drop. Competitors may introduce new, more innovative products.

A shorter product development cycle reduces the interval during which
market conditions can change while the product is being developed. As Figure
1–4 shows, the accuracy in estimating market conditions declines further in
the future, usually with a precipitous drop at some point. While the slope of
this curve varies, the shorter the time horizon, the greater the accuracy. A
shorter development cycle also enables a company to respond more rapidly to
emerging market opportunities. With product development flexibility, a company can be much more market oriented and respond much more quickly to
customer needs.

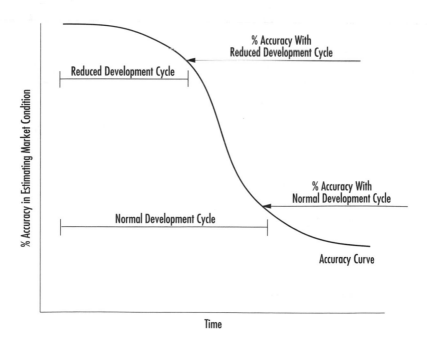

FIGURE 1–4   Increased accuracy in anticipating customer requirements
comes from faster time-to-market.

Improved Product Development Productivity

Product development productivity does not come from working people harder. Motivating developers to work day and night only temporarily increases capacity and can reduce overall effectiveness. Increased product development productivity is derived from shorter cycle times, less development waste, better resource utilization, and the ability to attract the best people. Again, the parallels to improvements in manufacturing should be obvious.

Shorter development cycle times

Most product development investments are run-rate based, meaning that a certain number of people work on a product development project until it is completed. For example, twenty people may work on developing a new product for three years. Development costs are highly correlated to cycle time: if the cycle time is reduced, development costs are lower. This is the same relationship between cost and cycle time that exists in manufacturing. The relationship between project cost and development cycle time is shown in Figure 1–5.

With an improved process, product development cycle time is reduced and project costs go down. In the previous example, if the project could be completed in one and one-half years (half the time), it would not require forty people (although it may require a few more than twenty to remove some constraints). Therefore, the project cost would be lower. This cost reduction, while related to the reduction in cycle time, is not directly proportional because other costs, such as capital equipment, tooling, and outside expenses, may not be reduced with shorter cycle time. We have found that a 50% reduction in product development cycle time typically leads to direct reduction of development costs of between 30% and 35%.

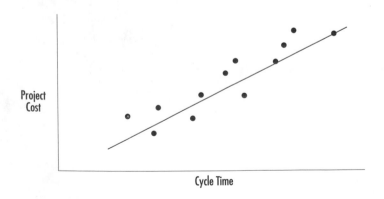

FIGURE 1–5   Relationship of product development cycle time and project cost.

The resources saved through increased productivity can be reinvested in additional product development projects to bring more new products to market, or a company can reduce the total amount of money it spends on developing new products. Some companies have combined these cycle-time/cost-reduction benefits by increasing development activity along with reducing the money they spend. Most have chosen to increase their new product output.

Less development waste

Some cancellation or significant redirection of product development projects is to be expected. However, too many projects are canceled or redirected quite late, after significant investments have been made. In most cases, cancellation or redirection could have taken place much earlier. The necessary information was either known or knowable, but nobody asked the right questions or made the right decisions.

Our benchmarks show that companies making earlier decisions waste significantly less on products that are not brought to market. The best-in-class companies waste only 1.1% by canceling product development projects after the planning and specification phase, while others waste 19.2%.[6] Put another way, companies with a better decision-making process can spend less on product development and achieve comparable output because they waste less on products that do not come to market.

Here is a case example. The Financial Products & Systems division of AT&T in Dundee, Scotland is the world's leader in ATMs (automated teller machines). Using PACE (Product And Cycle-time Excellence), it canceled a product development project that it previously would have begun developing, only to cancel later because the market was not ready. The estimated savings was $5 million.[7]

Better resource utilization

Companies often miss project milestones because key tasks are delayed while waiting for the right people to do them. Some projects are canceled well into development because the development resources are needed elsewhere. People bounce back and forth from project to project, with reduced effectiveness and an increase in coordination activity. Companies typically launch more product development projects than they have capacity for and then are surprised when projects fall behind schedule. Ineffective resource allocation is frequently the underlying cause.

Here again the analogy to manufacturing improvement applies. Traditional manufacturing management encouraged companies to launch as much work as possible so that the factory would be highly utilized. This led to bulging work-in-process inventory, schedule slippages, and increased overhead. Until the emphasis changed to cycle-time reduction, people lost sight of the fact that the goal was not to start as much as possible but to finish as much as possible.

Just as the implementation of just-in-time manufacturing clearly exposes production bottlenecks, the implementation of a high-performance product development process clearly exposes real resource needs and skill bottlenecks. Managing these constraints enables a company to set the priorities necessary to implement its strategy, match the mix of development resources to its needs, and increase overall productivity.

Better ability to attract and retain technical talent

The most capable and creative people are almost always the most productive. This is particularly true in product development, where creativity and skill are essential.

With a rapid and efficient product development process, a company is in a much better position to both attract and retain key development talent. Product development professionals, whether they are technical gurus or project managers, are attracted to a work environment in which their efforts more frequently result in successful new products. Such an environment allows them to work on more projects during their careers. Conversely, if they work in an environment where their efforts stretch out over a long period of time, they become frustrated and inevitably look for new work environments. Given the importance of exceptional technical talent in the product development process, attracting and retaining the best people can become a significant long-term advantage.

Operational Efficiencies

Improving product development can also achieve operational benefits — especially in manufacturing and service — by designing a product to make operations easier or more efficient. More predictable product completion dates also improve the efficiency and effectiveness of the product launch.

Design for manufacturability, serviceability, and so on

Operational efficiencies in manufacturing, distribution, and service can be achieved by better product design. This focus is typically incorporated in such design methods as design for manufacturing and assembly (DFMA), design for international (DFI), and design for serviceability (DFS). In the AT&T Financial Products & Systems division example introduced earlier, one new product developed under PACE achieved a 60% improvement in quality, as measured by defects at integration test.[8]

Higher-quality products

High product quality is an essential element of product excellence. Baldrige Award winner Motorola is noted for the success of its six-sigma quality program, a statistical term denoting 3.4 defects per million operations. Motorola's

Codex division implemented six-sigma as part of its improved product development process. Codex achieved this result by integrating specific quality requirements into all steps of a consistent design process and through a decision process that requires achievement of quality goals before a product is released. Codex actually delayed products that did not meet these stringent quality hurdles, even though the products were functioning and customers were awaiting delivery.

Lower engineering change order costs

The costs of implementing engineering change orders (ECOs) caused by design problems can frequently be higher than most companies realize. For example, one company estimated that 10% of its direct labor was involved in implementing ECOs. In some of our benchmarking, we found that more than half of the companies surveyed incurred ECO costs that were greater than 10% of the original development costs. ECOs are frequently caused by rushing a product to market rather than designing it properly.

ECOs can increase other costs as well. For example, the service costs caused by such problems can be enormous. One highly innovative blood-analyzer system introduced too early required replacement of parts and subsystems equal in cost to the selling price of the unit in all systems installed in the first year. At another company the sales force spent 80% of its time babysitting a new product. This kept current customers pacified, but was done at the expense of developing new customers.

The number of ECOs after product release is directly related to the quality of product design. The product development process drives the quality of product design through such practices as structured development, design reviews, and concurrent engineering.

Improved predictability of launch

Many operational activities take place just before and after the launch of a new product. These include market preparation activities, acquisition of components for the new product, and the phaseout of older products being replaced. Some of these activities require decisions to be made months or even a year or more before the new-product release date. The failure to accurately predict product release dates has caused a precipitous drop in revenue for some companies, which ended up unable to ship even the older products to customers.

In some cases, companies are forced to release products before they are ready. A manager at a company we know that had this problem put it this way: "Our products don't get launched; they escape!"

The benefits of reliable release dates vary by company and situation. If a company does not have confidence in the release date of a new product, it usually stocks up on additional inventory of older products — just in case. These are later written off if the new product is on schedule. If a company prepares its sales force — or worse, its customers — for a new product and then misses its expected release date, a significant revenue impact will occur. Lotus Software experienced this in 1985 when it missed its schedule for releasing Jazz, its integrated software product for the Macintosh.

Why Haven't Companies Already Achieved These Benefits?

Despite significant benefits and the fact that untapped opportunities like this are rare, some companies have not yet made measurable improvements to their product development process. That is why improving product development is a unique opportunity — one that can upset the competitive balance of many industries.

Why hasn't the product development process been improved? We believe that the answer is in one or more of the following reasons:

1. *Product development has not been viewed, managed, or taught as a process.* Traditionally, product development has been looked upon as an art — products were created by a mixture of genius and inspiration. It was not something that could be managed; it just happened.

Prior to the 1990s, much of the literature focused on the mysteries of creativity and human communication. This work implied that product development could not be managed, only a suitable climate provided. Yet, structure and active management needn't stifle innovation; they provide boundaries that focus creativity and empowerment based on clear-cut responsibilities. Structure doesn't impede product development. It merely clarifies the process; then the creativity starts.

Many companies delayed investing in improving their product development process because it was never managed as a process. In meetings with company executives, we asked the following questions after citing the benefits of improving the product development process:

- How much did you invest in improving your manufacturing process through manufacturing systems such as material requirements planning (MRP), techniques such as just-in-time (JIT) and total quality control (TQC), production process improvements such as production or manufacturing engineering, and training in process-improvement skills? The answers usually indicated that they had made significant investments in these areas.
- How much do you invest in improving the product development process through process engineering, implementing new techniques, organizational improvement, and training? The answer frequently was "little or none."

These executives quickly realized that they had not been investing in improving their most essential business process.

Product development is a process. Inputs such as market opportunities and technology go into the process, and products result. The process can be defined, structured, and managed. There are similarities from one development project to another, and like any process it can be continually improved. Most important, the competitor with a superior process has an advantage.

2. *The necessary concepts and techniques have only recently been developed.* The revolution in manufacturing required new concepts for managing manufacturing in a completely different way. Innovative methods such as just-in-time production, new philosophies such as total quality management and vendor partnering, and supporting techniques such as pull mechanisms and set-up time reduction provided the foundation for companies to implement this new manufacturing process.

The concepts, philosophies, and techniques for managing the product development process lag far behind those for manufacturing. Until the late 1980s, there were few advances in the process of developing products. PACE was developed as an integrated approach to product development to address this deficiency. It includes new management concepts, techniques, and frameworks for achieving high-performance product development.

3. *The improvement usually requires a cultural change.* Improving the product development process usually involves moving toward a performance-oriented approach in which the foci become teamwork, rapid decision making, and clear responsibility. This orientation presents a cultural change for many companies.

Cultural change, even when desired, is difficult to implement. It cuts across all functions horizontally and all levels vertically. Issuing edicts to effect improvements that require a completely different way of doing things rarely work. While cultural change usually evolves over time or comes as the result of an upheaval, successful companies have been able to change their culture to implement improvements. Hewlett Packard with JIT, and Motorola with quality are well-known examples of this type of cultural change. Because it is so difficult to achieve, however, it has stopped many companies that want to change the way they develop products.

4. *Cross-functional changes are difficult to make from within.* Product development is a cross-functional process, and not only are the improvements cross functional, but much of the emphasis is on lowering functional barriers. Companies that have attempted cross-functional change have found that it is difficult with internal initiatives.

If a vice president in one function leads the change, for example, then everyone believes that he or she is biased toward making tasks easier for his or her own function, and in many companies there is a long history of this actually happening. If the change is initiated by a multifunctional group or committee, they may get bogged down by many of the problems of group consensus. Frequently, outside assistance is necessary to successfully implement cross-functional change.

5. *The changes are too extensive.* The product development process is complex, and hundreds or even thousands of changes may be required to improve it. Most of them are small, but a few are very large. Nevertheless, they all need to be coordinated, since many are interdependent. Making the numerous changes and coordinating their implementation can overwhelm companies that are inexperienced or not sufficiently committed. They try, but fail, and the resulting frustration makes the situation even worse.

6. *Some companies mistakenly think that they have done it already.* The changes needed are both deep and subtle. Because of this, some companies are deceived into thinking the changes that they have made are sufficient while they have only touched the surface.

Competitive Advantage

Individually, the benefits of increased revenue, improved product development productivity, and operational efficiencies are compelling. Taken together they provide a significant competitive advantage. Companies able to achieve this advantage will grow faster, be more profitable, and succeed against competitors who can't.

The combined advantages open the possibility for new competitive strategies. A company with these advantages could inundate its competitors with new products. Toshiba attempted this strategy in 1990 by blitzing the laptop computer market with an avalanche of new products, addressing virtually every market niche. Faced with this onslaught, customers may consider competitors also-rans because their product development cycle is longer than the product life cycle established by Toshiba.[9]

Alternatively, a company with these advantages could profitably develop products that its competitors could only match at a loss, or it could choose to be significantly more profitable on the same level of new product investment. The strategic possibilities are many, and they will be the basis for the new competitive battles of the future.

These benefits are not theoretical. Companies are achieving them today. Almost any company can achieve them. Most executives that we talk to are disappointed in their product development process. Most, as revealed by our benchmarking studies, believe that their companies could reduce time-to-market by at least one-third.

Summary

There is a dramatic change taking place in product development, and this will alter the competitive balance of some industries for the following reasons:

- An improved product development process can increase revenue by increasing product life-cycle revenue, improving market penetration, enabling success in time-sensitive markets, and creating more successful products.
- An improved product development process can increase productivity by shortening development cycle times, reducing wasted development, improving resource utilization, and attracting technical talent.
- It can also improve other operational efficiencies by incorporating design for manufacturability, encouraging higher-quality products, reducing the number of ECOs, and improving the predictability of release.
- Achieved together, the benefits of an improved product development process can establish a significant competitive advantage.
- The magnitude of improvement is significant — for example, most companies can cut time-to-market in half.
- Product development remains an untapped opportunity, mainly because it has not been effectively managed as a process and is very difficult to change.

References

1. Pittiglio Rabin Todd & McGrath, *Product Development Leadership for Technology-Based Companies*, 1995 Benchmarking Study of product development in 220 high-technology companies.

2. Rick Whiting, "Product Development as a Process," *Electronic Business* (June 17, 1991).

3. *BBN Communications News Release* (October 8, 1991): 4.

4. Pittiglio Rabin Todd & McGrath, *Product Development Leadership for Technology-Based Companies*, 1995 Benchmarking Study of product development in 220 high-technology companies.

5. Rick Whiting, "Product Development as a Process," *Electronic Business* (June 17, 1991): 31.

6. Pittiglio Rabin Todd & McGrath, *Product Development Leadership for Technology-Based Companies*, 1995 Benchmarking Study of product development in 220 high-technology companies.

7. Dean Gilmore and Jim Leighton, "Keeping one PACE ahead of the competition," *Engineering Management Journal* (April 1995).

8. Ibid.

9. Gary Hamel and C. K. Prahalad, "Corporate Imagination and Expeditionary Marketing," *Harvard Business Review* (July–August 1991).

CHAPTER 2

PACE: An Integrated Process for Product And Cycle-time Excellence

Michael E. McGrath
Cindy L. Akiyama

The only sustainable source of product advantage is a superior product development process. Advantages based on a brilliant design, fortunate timing, a competitor's misstep, or a lucky break cannot be sustained. Such factors cannot be relied upon to consistently create successful products over the long term. An inferior development process will make advantages based on such factors short-lived. A superior process will consistently identify the best product opportunities, define competitive products, and bring them to market faster.

Product development is a process. It takes insights into customer needs and wants, combines them with the company's technologies and skills, and then transforms opportunities into products. Usually, the process can be similar for all products developed within a company. Although there are product differences, the approach to project-team organization, project management, decision making, planning, and indeed the approach to many of the specific steps can be consistent. In fact, there can even be a high degree of similarity in the product development process from company to company.

This similarity enables the product development process to be structured, defined, and managed. As with other business processes, a high-level process can be designed so that each project team is not required to invent its own. Investments can then be made in improving the process so that all projects reap its benefits. Best practices can be applied across many companies and a general structure for product development can be tailored to each.

Pittiglio Rabin Todd & McGrath (PRTM)'s Product And Cycle-time Excellence (PACE) is a process reference model for product development. It is a proven approach based on extensive experience and an understanding of best practices. PACE integrates the major elements that are essential to product development and addresses the deficiencies that exist in many product development processes today.

The Product Development Process — Seven Elements

The process for product development can be segmented into seven interrelated elements, each with its own common pitfalls. PACE provides the approaches, techniques, and methods for overcoming deficiencies in each of these elements. The following section provides a description of the seven interrelated elements of the product development process, a summary of some of the common deficiencies, and a brief description of the PACE approach for that element. Each PACE element is described in more detail in a subsequent chapter.

Decision Making

All companies have a decision-making process for new products, although they may not recognize it as an explicitly defined process. Where the decision-making process is weak, delays due to indecision are common. For example, when the de facto process is serial, requiring many managers to be individually convinced of a product concept's merit, start-up delays can result. We have seen good opportunities ignored simply because the product champions didn't understand how to make the informal decision-making process work.

One computer company with which we worked had an ineffective decision-making process that was typical of many processes we have seen. Project reviews had deteriorated to a series of lengthy presentations to varied audiences. Many people attended and asked numerous questions, but these were not decision-making sessions. The reviews were not given at the right point in the development process to make decisions and the right information was not presented to facilitate decision making. Senior management avoided the reviews and there were no other mechanisms to force timely decisions.

However, not all explicitly defined decision-making processes are effective. Some are poorly designed or have not been properly implemented. In such cases, a formal process can actually be an administrative hindrance to product development. Instead of becoming the beat that drives product development, the decision-making process consumes an extensive amount of time with little benefit.

In our reviews of product development, we have seen problems such as the following due to inadequate decision-making processes:

- Senior management unconsciously delays or revises decisions because it doesn't know who should make the decision or what type of consensus is needed.
- Poor decisions result from inadequate information or inappropriate level of detail.
- The right questions are not answered at the right time.
- Decision points are not defined so that reviews occur at the appropriate milestones.
- Resources are over-committed to the point that it becomes impossible to get anything done on schedule.
- Funding for product development projects is not clearly approved by those authorized to approve new products and set priorities.
- Decisions are made too late — frequently after the product is already designed.
- Cycle-time guidelines are not used to validate project schedules.
- Strategic decisions are made in frustration by developers because senior management has not made them.

In the PACE process, new product decision making is implemented through a Phase Review Process that requires decisions at specifically defined points during development. A product development project must achieve clearly defined objectives in the expected time frame in order to get approval to continue into the next phase.

Product Approval Committee (PAC) is a term used to describe the senior management group within a division or company that has the specific authority and responsibility to make major new product decisions. The PAC has the authority to approve or reject new products by funding or modifying them at specific decision points in the development cycle. It is responsible for implementing the company's strategy through product development activities and therefore has the resource-allocation authority to drive new product development.

The PAC makes decisions and allocates resources through the Phase Review Process. Without such a process, it is virtually impossible for senior management to effectively guide new product development. Simply having a review process (or something similar such as a tollgate process or stage-development process), however, is not enough. A poor definition, improper implementation, or incompatibility with other necessary elements of the development process can make the review process ineffective.

The Phase Review Process plays another important role in product development. Through it the PAC directly and unambiguously empowers the project team to develop the product on a phase-by-phase basis. The project team defines its recommendations for the product, presents a plan to develop it, and requests the resources required for the next phase of development. If the PAC approves the team's recommendations, it empowers the team with the authority, responsibility, and resources required to implement the next phase of the team's plan.

Project Team Organization

In our reviews, we found that while most companies had formal project teams, many were not successful. Generally, the project team's structure, roles, and responsibilities were not clearly defined. As a result, communication, coordination, and decision making were inefficient and confused.

One company typified this, with numerous managers participating in product development team meetings only when they had the time or when a specific issue made it a priority. Because this approach created poor results, the company tried to fix it in different ways. A program management department was established to monitor schedules and commitments, in order to identify who was supposed to do what and whether it was done. Later, each function assigned its own project manager to every major project. Neither of these approaches worked very well. They only increased non-value-added effort, which was already too high.

Companies have established project team organizations, but many have not been effective. The following are typical reasons that we have seen for this lack of success:

- Confusion results when the responsibilities and authorities of project teams and functional organizations are not clearly defined.
- Teams are ineffective because they are not really empowered to accomplish the objectives; in some cases they are given the responsibility but not the authority or resources.
- Concurrent engineering is lacking because some functions and skills are not properly integrated into the team's activities.
- Project leadership is ineffective, stemming from several factors: inexperienced project leaders, a weakly defined role for project leadership, inadequate training, rotating team leadership, or a flawed definition of the project team organization.
- Project teams cannot achieve results because they lack the staff and skills to do it; frequently, resources are moved from team to team without any clear decision.
- Conflict and confusion arise between the project team and the functional organization because the way in which they work together is not clearly defined.
- Ineffective teams result from confusion over what the members are supposed to do; for example, team members think that they are functional reviewers or note-takers and not actual contributors making real-time decisions.

Project team organization is an essential element of the product development process. An effective project team vastly improves communication, coordination, and decision making. Early in our reviews we found that many of the popular project team approaches were ineffective in ways similar to those described above. We developed a new approach that took the best aspects of established project team organizational approaches while overcoming their drawbacks. We have called it the Core Team approach to project team organization.

A Core Team is a small cross-functional project team that has authority to develop a specific product. A typical Core Team has five to eight members with the authority and responsibility to manage all of the tasks associated with developing the product. These specific tasks are divided among the Core Team members, and each performs these tasks using staff assigned to the project. Core Team members do this by directing the work of those assigned to them, interfacing with functional areas, and collectively making decisions as part of the Core Team. The PAC empowers the Core Team with this responsibility and authority at each phase of the development effort through the Phase Review Process. Each Core Team has a leader who guides and directs the team. The team executes each development phase in accordance with a "contract" with the PAC that defines key project targets and allowed variances.

Development Activity Structure

Development activity is the actual work that takes place to develop a new product. In PACE, the structured development process defines what activities should be done, their sequence, their interdependencies, and the standard terminology used for development. In our reviews we found three general categories of deficiencies in the structure of development activity: (1) companies without any defined structure for product development, (2) those with detailed procedure manuals that weren't followed, and (3) those with a structured process that did not improve or speed development.

In the first case, companies must repeatedly "reinvent the wheel" during product development. Each project team is expected to define the process that it will follow, and as a result, each project team does development differently, even if it is performing the same or similar tasks. This approach lengthens development cycles and project teams throughout the company are prone to make the same mistakes.

In the second case, the process is documented, but not followed. Typically, a staff person has defined the development process in a procedure book and issued the book with the naive expectation that everyone will follow it. Of course they don't, and in most cases it is better that they don't. Project teams again put in place their own product development process.

In the third case, development activities are defined and followed, but the process is inherently inefficient. Surprisingly, when they formalize their process, many companies simply document what they are already doing, even if it is ineffective. As a result, they institutionalize their problems.

In our reviews of development activity, we find the following deficiencies to be common:

- Continuous revision of products resulting from undisciplined development activity.

- Inadequate project planning and preparation caused by misunderstanding of what activities must be completed and by when.
- Poor execution of development stemming directly from a lack of common terminology and the understanding that it brings.
- Definition of product development activity so detailed that it makes development inefficient — typically the definition lacks structure.
- Slow development resulting from a bureaucratic process with multiple sign-offs at every step.
- A lack of concurrent engineering because it is not designed into the structured development process.
- Inaccurate project schedules resulting from a lack of cycle-time guidelines for development activities.
- Failure to continuously improve the product development process because the responsibility for it has not been assigned.

Within PACE, the Core Team develops a product using a structured development process that ensures consistency and avoids the need for each project team to invent its own process. A common structured process also enables the use of common cycle-time guidelines and provides a foundation for continuous improvement.

In the PACE approach, a structured development process consists of several levels. Within the framework provided by the Phase Review Process, there are typically fifteen to twenty major steps that define a company's process for developing products. Each of these steps is then broken into ten to thirty tasks that define how each step is done within the company. The tasks define standard cycle times for each step so that the steps can be used as building blocks for scheduling, estimating resource requirements, planning, and management.

Each task may be further broken down into various activities. The number of activities within each step varies from several to as many as thirty or forty, according to the nature of the task. Generally, steps and tasks apply consistently from project to project, while activities tend to be project-specific.

Development Tools and Techniques

Design techniques such as quality function deployment (QFD), design for assembly (DFA), and design for manufacturability (DFM) can enhance the success of a product and achieve related operating efficiencies. None of these techniques alone, however, will solve all product development issues.

One large, multidivisional high-technology company, for example, selected QFD as its ultimate solution. It invested heavily to train the entire company in the design technique. Internal QFD experts and advisors were developed to spread the gospel. After nine months with no improvement in product development, the group was dissolved. The QFD technique was unfairly blamed because people expected a technique to make up for the lack of an overall integrated approach.

During the past five to ten years, a number of new automated design tools have been developed that can significantly aid the product development process. These include computer aided engineering (CAE), object-oriented software development tools, product data management systems, simulation tools, and tools for project planning, scheduling, and decision making. Again, no one alone provides a complete solution. Each can help make a process more productive, but all require a framing process as a prerequisite.

Regarding the use of these techniques and tools, we have found that many companies err in one of two ways: either they are not applying the right techniques and tools, or they are applying them ineffectively because they do not have an overall product development process. Specifically, we see the following problems to be common:

- Design techniques are ineffective because they don't fit into a clear product development process.
- A particular design technique such as QFD is expected to solve all product development problems.
- New products are not manufacturable or serviceable because the proper design techniques are not used.
- Product development takes longer than it should because automated tools are not being applied.
- Automated development tools don't yield expected results because the product definition keeps changing.

The PACE process does not define new techniques or tools; the focus within PACE is on applying the right technique or tool, at the right time, and within the context of an overall product development process. It outlines a number of design techniques and automated development tools and shows how they fit into the process.

Product Strategy Process

Product strategy is the starting point for the development of new products. Through product strategy, a company defines the types of products it wants to develop, how it will differentiate its products from those of its competitors, how it will introduce new technology into its products, and what priorities it will establish for developing new products.

Products selected for development should be consistent with the overall product strategy, but often this is not the case. Frequently, the product strategy has not been clearly defined and articulated, even though there may have been informal discussions throughout the organization. Without a clear product strategy, developers must make guesses about it as they propose new products and execute development projects. They learn what fits and what doesn't by trial and error.

Sometimes the disconnection between product strategy and development projects is so profound that the former is a wish list without any impact on actual project selection. At one company, the overriding strategic objective was to develop many new products. Without more guidance than that, or some framework for evaluating product ideas and setting priorities, dozens of projects were started simultaneously on the initiative of individual developers or their managers. Most of these projects were never completed or, despite technical success, were never commercialized. "If I'd known what they were working on," the CEO told us, "I'd have stopped them sooner. Most of their projects didn't fit our strategy."

Our experience has shown the following typical deficiencies in setting and communicating product strategy:

- Companies focus too much on individual products and not enough on product platforms.
- Nobody in the company has the clear responsibility for product strategy.
- Since there is no formal process for product strategy, it tends to be done superficially as part of the annual budgeting process.
- Mediocre products are developed because the company does not effectively evaluate its strategic opportunities.
- A product strategy is outdated because it focuses on today's needs, not future customer needs and market trends.
- Noncompetitive products result from a product strategy that is internally, not customer, driven; competitive analysis is shallow and competitive positioning is unclear.
- Actual product development differs from what was intended because there is no product strategy vision to guide those working on development projects.

Contrary to popular belief, the best product strategies are not derived from blinding flashes of innovation. Nor do they arise from hundreds of pages of market analysis, complete with charts and graphs. Digital Equipment Corporation, for example, outlined one of the most successful product strategies in computer history with a three-page memo defining the future architecture of the VAX platform. Effective product strategy arises from a rigorous process for defining product plans based on understanding the opportunities created by the intersection of changes in the marketplace, advances in technology, and competitive positioning.

Within PACE, product strategy provides the framework used by the PAC to make decisions and set priorities in the Phase Review Process; it also establishes guidelines for Core Teams to use in defining products. Product strategy includes defining the opportunities for expanding existing product lines and creating new product lines.

Although specific product strategy varies by company — based on their approach to business strategy, their organization, their industry and competitive position, and so on — product strategy can be managed as a process. The PACE product strategy element defines this process.

Technology Management

Technology management is part of the overall product development process. The function of technology management is to identify opportunities for applying new technology, and initiate technology-development projects that further the company's core competencies and benefit multiple products.

We have found that many technology-based companies do not proactively manage their underlying technologies. Some companies become so focused on product development that they end up developing technology as subprojects within product development. Many of the troubled development projects we reviewed ran into technical difficulties because the companies didn't realize that they lacked the fundamental technical expertise needed to develop the products.

Product development relies on technology, whether internally developed, licensed, or otherwise acquired from outside the organization. Timely access to usable technology requires identification of present and future core technologies, because developing technology and building technology alliances takes time. This cannot be done by forcing development project teams to create or acquire the necessary core technologies while they are developing a product. The degree of risk in a development project is determined by its riskiest indispensable element. If that element is core technology development, the uncertainty and potential delay can be enormous.

One company, for example, didn't understand technology management. R&D was working on many varied technologies to be useful "three to ten years from now." Yet most of this work did not make the best use of the company's existing technology base. Consequently, its core technologies matured without replacement. Starved for research dollars, core technologies critical to the product line became obsolete and, while losing market share, the company had to invest heavily to catch up.

In our reviews of product development, we find the following deficiencies in technology management to be common:

- Product development delays caused by technical surprises that could have been avoided through better technical preparation.
- Deterioration of technical competencies because the company fails to invest in current and future core technologies.
- Unnecessarily long development cycles because technology development is not decoupled from product development.
- Project failures caused by inadequate management of technology risk.

The technology management element within PACE defines the process for technology development and the transfer of technology to product development. It clarifies the distinction between product development and technology development and defines the link to product strategy.

Pipeline Management

Finally, the need for better management across all product development projects becomes apparent after companies have eliminated deficiencies in the project-based aspects of product development. As contention for scarce resources across projects becomes apparent, pipeline management becomes the next priority.

We find several common issues that are addressed by pipeline management:

- Development project delays stemming from over-allocated resources — frequently this is caused by an ineffective resource scheduling system.
- Fire-fighting decisions made without the context of project priorities.
- Functional budgets misaligned with project resource assignments.
- Misalignment between project skill requirements and departmental resources.
- Product development decisions not made with consideration of company objectives for growth, product mix, or short- and long-range emphasis.

These issues apply to all product development projects and need to be properly managed across them. The PACE pipeline management element addresses these issues by providing a framework for project prioritization, cross-project resource management, and aligning functional capabilities and project requirements.

The PACE Architecture

PACE is both a goal and a blueprint, or reference model, for the product development process. It defines product development as an integrated process in which subprocesses, organizational structures, development activities, techniques, and tools work together within a single overall framework. The PACE architecture can be viewed as seven interrelated elements that are grouped along two dimensions: project management and cross-project management.

The four project management elements illustrated in Figure 2–1 (the Phase Review Process, Core Teams, structured development process, and development tools & techniques) form the basic foundation of PACE. These elements are required for each product development project. Mastering these elements enables a company to reduce time-to-market, accurately schedule project completion, increase R&D productivity, and reduce the investment in products that don't go to market. We equate implementation of these elements with Stage 2 in the evolution of the product development process that is described in Chapter 10.

While these elements can be described separately, they are only effective within the framework of the total process. The success of any one element depends on others within the overall product development process. Core Teams, for example, can only be effective if they are truly empowered. Without the decision making that comes from the Phase Review Process, teams cannot truly be empowered, and their levels of responsibility and authority can become confused.

Likewise, if senior management makes the best possible decisions and the organization does not effectively implement them, new product development will fail. Core Teams or similar high-performance teams are essential to implementing cross-functional requirements.

No matter how talented, a Core Team will take significantly longer to develop a product if it needs to reinvent the development steps involved for each new product. A common structured development process also enables the Core Team to build on lessons learned from past projects so that mistakes are not repeated.

Techniques such as QFD and DFM cannot truly be effective without a context in which to use them. QFD requires both a team to perform it and a process that defines when it should be applied. DFM requires early involvement of manufacturing in product design, which in turn requires a team organization to make it work. Tools that automate the development process have proven to be less than effective if the process itself is not clearly defined. This

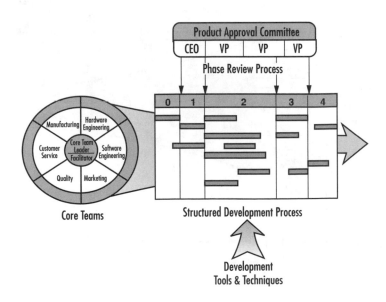

FIGURE 2–1 The four project management elements of PACE.

is similar to manufacturing, wherein many companies invested heavily in automated equipment such as material handling and high-speed manufacturing systems, only to subsequently learn that just-in-time manufacturing and set-up time reduction eliminated the need for this investment. The message is the same: the process needs to be structured and simplified before automation can be truly effective.

After mastering the project management elements, a company usually raises new questions. How do we identify the best product opportunities? How do we better integrate technology development? How do we balance resources strategically and tactically across all projects in our portfolio? The next three elements: product strategy, technology management, and pipeline management, provide the infrastructure necessary to manage the product development portfolio and integrate it within the enterprise as a whole. These cross-project management elements are illustrated in Figure 2–2.

Many companies have improved one or more specific elements of their development process, only to be disappointed with the overall results. Piecemeal improvements often lead to increased frustration and a sense that "we've already tried that." There is no magic bullet. A dramatic increase in new product development performance results from a coordinated set of integrated process improvements that mutually support and reinforce one another.

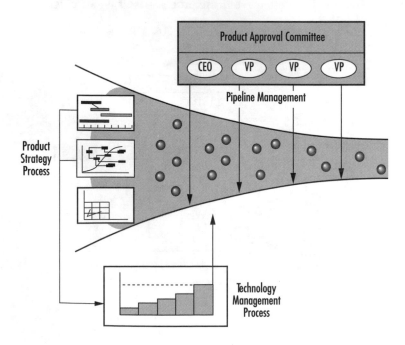

FIGURE 2–2   Cross-project management elements.

PACE is not just theory. It is an approach proven by more than ten years of successful implementation in more than a hundred companies. Public interviews with companies that have implemented PACE demonstrate this.

- "This is the real stuff; this isn't theory," claims Michael P. LaVigna, president of Bolt, Beranek and Newman, a Cambridge, Massachusetts manufacturer of computers, software, and communications equipment. "I can't imagine companies today doing product development without this process," he said, referring to the PACE process.[1]
- Parry Norling, planning director, Corporate R&D labs at Du Pont: "What PACE does is get the business involved at the very start. When R&D is through with a product, the business has already decided to sell it, so we've cut some 40% to 60% off the time of getting new products to market, because the strategic thinking and commercialization decisions have been made ahead of time. Innovation becomes a business process, not a research process." Currently about half the businesses at Du Pont are using the PACE process for new-product innovation.[2]
- The Codex division of Motorola chopped its average product development time by 46%, while developing and shipping more products than at any other time in the company's history. In terms of quality, Richard P. Schroeder, formerly corporate quality assurance vice president, says that "New products have reached a sigma quality level of 5.5 to 5.7 (approximately ten defects per million operations)."[3]
- Prior to PACE, Thomson Consumer Electronics' product development had never moved along very precisely. "We had modifications of the modifications," moans Erich A. Geiger, executive vice president of R&D.[4]

Unique Aspects of PACE

Some companies have defined PACE-like processes, but have not derived the magnitude of benefits achieved by those who have implemented PACE. Why is this? The answer lies in unique aspects of the PACE elements:

- The PACE Phase Review Process provides specific tools and approaches that enable crisp, timely, well-communicated decision making and delegation.
- Subtleties of the PACE Core Team approach to project organization enable a team to function like a "start-up" company while taking advantage of the skills and infrastructure of a larger organization.
- The structured development process optimizes the scope and content of process documentation to each intended audience; it enables project schedules to mirror the development process.

- PACE enables the right development tools and techniques to be applied at the right time and within the context of an overall development process.
- Within PACE, product strategy is a management process.
- The PACE technology management process ensures that core technologies are identified, actively managed, and integrated with product development activities.
- Pipeline management provides a framework and tool set for managing activities that must be integrated across all development projects; it links the product development cycle to the annual planning cycle.

In summary, nuances of *how* PACE's seven interrelated elements are implemented can drive the difference between a best-in-class product development process and one that is bureaucratic, circumvented, and ineffective in bringing competitive products to market.

References

1. Rick Whiting, "Product Development as a Process," *Electronic Business* (June 17, 1991): 32.
2. Tim Stevens, "Tool Kit For Innovators," *Industry Week* (June 5, 1995).
3. "Three Companies That Have Seen the Light of Product Development," *Electronic Business* (June 17, 1991): 68.
4. Barbara N. Berkman, "Thomson Fine-Tunes Its HDTV Picture," *Electronic Business* (June 17, 1991): 85.

CHAPTER 3

The Phase Review Process and Effective Decision Making

Michael E. McGrath

Product development is driven by the decision-making process that determines what products to develop and how development resources are assigned. Through this process, senior management leads product development, implements product strategy, and empowers project teams to develop new products.

Despite its importance, this decision-making process is often ineffective and may even slow down rather than drive development. Late decisions waste precious resources. Indecision causes projects to drift and delays their time-to-market. Lack of consensus leads to frequent product changes. Scarce resources are over-allocated, creating continuous delays and frustration.

Product development decision making is more than simply investing in any reasonably good idea with a projected return on investment above a targeted level. Most companies have ample new product opportunities; selecting from among many possibilities is the real challenge. This requires executing product strategy through product development decisions.

New product decisions are interdependent; going ahead with one project takes away resources that could be used on another and opens up possibilities for subsequent products. Limited resources means that priority decisions need to be made among products — and even within a specific new product, a choice needs to be made among alternative implementations.

In most cases, the fault lies not with the capability of senior management but with the decision-making process itself. Specifically, most companies do not have an effective decision-making process. Simply having a written policy or formal process is not enough; many companies that claim to have a project review process, for example, do not really use it to make timely decisions. When this critical decision-making process is ineffective, people throughout the company conclude that senior management does not know how to lead product development. Frequently the real problem is the lack of the appropriate process for senior managers to do their job — an effective Phase Review Process.

Ineffective decision making is expensive. Our benchmarking shows that the estimated cost of wasted development due to poor decision making is surprisingly high.

The Phase Review Process is the element within the PACE process that enables effective product development decisions and drives the rest of the process. These decisions are made by senior management (referred to as the Product Approval Committee, or PAC) designated with the authority and responsibility to make them. Phase reviews are decision-making sessions that occur at specific milestones in the product development process, and for each of these milestones there are clear expectations. Projects need to fulfill these expectations in order to continue.

The Role of Senior Management in Product Development

While everyone knows that senior management must lead product development, the question is: How does senior management actually do this? One executive shared his frustration in answering this question when he told us of the day he awoke with the renewed desire to lead his company to develop the best possible products. He arrived at his office that morning full of enthusiasm but didn't know where to start. He knew that leadership required more than solving problems related to completing products that were behind schedule. So he went to the lab and began to work with the engineers, giving them the benefit of his advice. He quickly realized that he was no longer as capable as the engineers at the job they were doing. So then he went to marketing and asked the people there what they saw as the opportunity for new products. Eventually he was so inundated with data that he got frustrated. At the end of the day, he called for a status review by all project leaders.

The next day at the review he was briefed on all fourteen active projects but had difficulty understanding any of them. The status reporting and formats were different. Too much status assessment relied on opinion, and all had excuses for why they were behind. They all asked that he get involved in resolving disputes among functional heads. At the end of the day, he threw up his hands, went home, and concluded that he didn't really know what his role should be in product development.

This case is all too common. Senior management may have the best intentions, but it frequently does not know what to do, when to do it, or how to do it. In contrast, successful leaders clearly know what to do. We have found that there are several actions that these leaders have in common.

1. *Establish the vision.* Some companies get the roles confused. Senior management gets involved in the detailed product design, leaving the designers with the need to set the product strategy. The preferred role of senior management is to set strategy by establishing the vision for the company's products. With a clear vision, the entire company can execute development activities to achieve it. Gordon Bell and Ken Olsen did this at Digital in the early 1970s with their vision of a common integrated architecture throughout the VAX product line. Jim Treybig did this at Tandem by establishing "the onlys," the things that only Tandem's computers can do.

2. *Make decisions.* Today, industry wastes hundreds of millions of dollars making product development decisions too late. Many companies decide to cancel or refocus a product development effort based on information that was actually known, or knowable, much earlier. One very large company estimated that it could save as much as $280 million per year by making decisions earlier in the development process.

The reason for poor decision making is not incompetence. As was stated earlier, it is because there is not an effective process that enables senior management to do its job and make the necessary decisions. Senior management needs to review the right information at the right time to make the right decision. For example, a project team may present a complete design and even a model for a product, but the team may not yet have identified the product's basic competitive differentiation. At this point it is almost impossible for senior management to conduct the necessary review to make the right decision.

3. *Cultivate the product development process.* A superior product development process can be a source of competitive advantage. While senior management cannot be involved in the details of all product development efforts, it can foster and cultivate the process for developing new products. This permits it to leverage its experience across all projects. It can invest in the product development process and set objectives for its continuous improvement. By supporting a common process, it smoothes execution of product development activities.

4. *Motivate.* In some companies, product development teams go home every day at 5:05 P.M., while at other companies they are there all night if necessary. Some development people have little respect for their senior management, while others will make any personal sacrifice necessary. The difference is in how successful senior management is in motivating its development staff. Successful motivation and leadership in product development require that senior management has already achieved respect in the three previous roles. If management has not established a vision, if it cannot make good decisions, or if it does not understand the development process, then it cannot get the respect of the development staff that it intends to motivate.

5. *Recruit the best development staff.* Senior management can play an important role in recruiting the best product development staff. This is especially important when trying to attract someone with a unique technical skill or exceptional product development track record. To do this successfully, however, senior management must first understand what skills must be added before they are needed. When management understands what is required, it can initiate and get involved in the recruiting efforts.

Senior management also needs to know when to get involved. In our experience, senior management is most typically involved in new product development toward the end, when products are ready to be released. It gets directly involved in fighting fires on products that are late or have problems. Unfortunately, by this time most of the decisions have been made, and the real impact of its involvement is minimal.

Even worse, management involvement frequently hinders problem resolution. Late in development the key individuals are lower-level engineers and technicians who can solve technical problems. Unfortunately, these are the people pulled away from their work to explain the problem to management, offer solutions, and wait for decisions.

The most effective time for senior management to be heavily involved in product development is up front, when strategic decisions are made and project direction is set. As the development project proceeds, resources are added and the work becomes progressively more detailed. Senior management's level of involvement should decrease accordingly as the ability to affect the product lessens. This is illustrated in Figure 3–1.

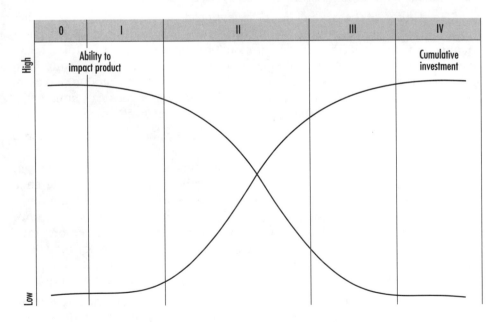

FIGURE 3–1   Management impact and resource involvement by phase.

Without a decision-making process, management will get involved in product development as it gets dragged into resolving crises and conflicts. With an effective decision-making process, it is compelled to make specific decisions at the appropriate project milestones.

Cost of Late Decisions

Without an effective process, decisions to cancel or redirect projects are often made too late. What is the cost of these late decisions? While almost everyone experienced with product development intuitively understands that decisions should be made as early as possible, benchmark data have shown that early decision making is even more significant than most managers realize. Table 3-1 compares the cancellation pattern in one company to those of other companies considered to be the best in their industry. For purposes of simplicity in illustrating the differences in timing, we assume that in each case 100 projects are initiated, that the overall success rate is the same (48% of all projects started), and that the investment in each project is $1 million. The distribution of the investment by phase is computed from benchmark studies for this industry.

TABLE 3–1 Lost investment due to development-project cancellation at various phases (in thousands of dollars).

	Phase 0	Phase 1	Phase II	Phase III	Phase IV	Total
Cumulative Investment	$75	$175	$780	$920	$1,000	
BEST COMPANIES						
Projects Active	100	70	56	56	50	48
% Canceled	30%	20%	0%	10%	5%	
No. Canceled	30	14	0	5.6	2.5	
Lost Invest ($000)	$2,250	$2,450	$0	$5,152	$2,520	$12,372
Total Invest ($000)						$60,372
CASE EXAMPLE						
Projects Active	100	90	77	57	50	48
% Canceled	10%	15%	25%	12.5%	5%	
No. Canceled	10	13.5	19.1	7.2	2.5	
Lost Invest ($000)	$750	$2,363	$14,918	$6,598	$2,510	$27,138
Total Invest ($000)						$75,138

Because of more effective decision making, the best companies cancel 30% of their projects after Phase 0, while the case-example company canceled only 10% at that stage. The total cost of these cancellations for the best companies compared to the case-example company was $2,250,000 versus $750,000. At the end of Phase I the best-company cancellation rate was again higher — 20% compared to 15%.

But Phase II is generally where most of the development investment is made. At the end of this phase the best companies had no canceled projects, while the case-example company canceled 25% of its projects. The cost of these cancellations amounted to almost $15 million.

By the end of development, each company had successfully completed 48 out of 100 projects originally started, with a total investment of $48 million for the successful projects. But the best companies wrote off only $12 million in canceled projects (20% of the $60 million total), while the case-example company wrote off $27 million (36% of the $75 million total). In other words, the best-practice companies developed 48 products at a cost of $60 million, while it cost the case-example company $75 million — 25% more. At that rate, the best-practice companies would be able to develop twelve additional products for the same amount of money.

Product Approval Committee

Within PACE, senior management involvement is channeled through a formally designated product approval group. Typically this is referred to as the Product Approval Committee (PAC), although different names, such as Product Review Board or new-product executive group, may be used. In some cases it is the company's executive committee.

The PAC is designated within the company to approve and prioritize new product development investments. Specifically, it has the authority and responsibility to do the following:

- Initiate new product development projects.
- Cancel and reprioritize projects.
- Ensure that products being developed fit the company's strategy.
- Allocate development resources.

Because the PAC is a decision-making group, it should remain small. Four to five executives is an appropriate size. It typically includes the CEO/COO/ General Manager, Marketing VP, R&D VP, VP of Finance, and Operations VP. Other senior executives may attend the phase reviews but do not maintain direct responsibility for new product development. PAC responsibilities typically require 10%–15% of a PAC member's time. This is a reasonable amount of time to spend in overseeing product development, and if the Phase Review Process is effective, it is an excellent use of time.

BBN Communications Corporation formed a product review board that consisted of the president and vice presidents of manufacturing, hardware and software development, and marketing. The product review board examined development projects at the conclusion of each phase and determined whether or not work should proceed. Ean Rankin, the division president, described the meetings as highly charged, with a tremendous amount of poking and prodding during the reviews because that is the time to find weaknesses in new products. The product review board made its decisions in a closed-door session and canceled several projects and redirected others. One of the major benefits of the product review board and Phase Review Process at BBN was that management had greater confidence in the decisions that it made.[1]

The Phase Review Process

The Phase Review Process drives the other product development processes within PACE. It is the process wherein senior management makes the difficult strategic-level product decisions, allocates resources to product development efforts, and provides direction and leadership to the project teams. These decisions are made through approval or cancellation at the conclusion of specific phases in the development effort.

The Phase Review Process is intended to cover all significant product development efforts, including all major new product development opportunities. Also, projects that have a significant impact on multiple functional areas, such as manufacturing, support, sales, and marketing, should be included in this process. Very small projects such as minor enhancements are usually managed by a simpler process or grouped and managed as a package.

The Phase Review Process can be viewed as a funnel (Figure 3–2), with many ideas entering at the concept phase and, through a series of screening decisions over the course of development, narrowed to a few appropriately resourced projects with a high likelihood of market success.[2] At the conclusion of each phase of development, a phase review is held to determine the direction of the project: proceed, cancel, or redirect.

In Phase 0 a product concept is pulled together by a few people (usually a combination of marketing and engineering) in a short time. Since only a small amount of effort is invested, a company can afford to review many concepts, thus promoting creativity. During Phase I more people work on the project for four to twelve weeks to develop specifications and lay out a detailed development plan. With detailed planning completed, the PAC can now weed out additional projects that are not attractive enough or cannot be resourced sufficiently. Beyond the Phase I review the funnel should become quite straight because significant resources will be committed to the project.

Phase reviews should be decision-making sessions and not briefings or presentations. The PAC should make a clear decision at the end of each review and communicate it clearly. This decision process should replace any procedures based on sign-offs.

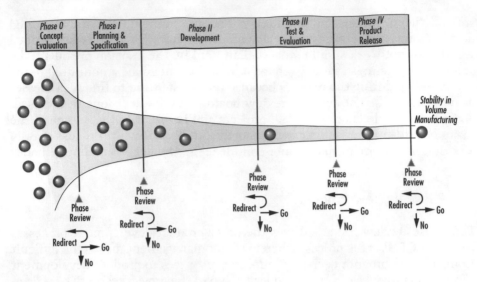

FIGURE 3–2   Phase review process funnel.

At each phase review, actual performance is compared to plan. Critical product and project characteristics such as the following are reviewed at each phase to assure performance and consistent direction:

- Progress to schedule
- Critical performance metrics
- Projected product cost, margin, revenue, life-cycle cost
- Development program budget and schedule
- Important market, competition, and industry information

Within PACE, the project team (Core Team) is empowered by the PAC at each phase review to execute the plan for the next phase. As long as the Core Team stays within agreed-upon tolerances, the PAC does not need to be involved in managing the development effort at a more detailed level. If major deviations occur during a phase, empowerment is automatically removed, and the Core Team leader is responsible for initiating an interim phase review to resolve the new situation. The Core Team is also responsible for devising a solution and for reviewing the proposed solution with the PAC.

The PAC approves funding for all resources on a phase-by-phase basis throughout the product development process. A project would not receive funding for the entire year but only for the next phase. A phase that covers multiple fiscal years would receive funding for the entire phase spanning those years. It is also necessary to take all authorized projects and relate them to the operating budgets and critical resources in a prioritized way so that the PAC knows how much can be allocated. If the funds or specific key resources are fully allocated, the PAC must prioritize project efforts to approve funding for the new project.

An effective Phase Review Process exhibits five major characteristics:

1. *Provide a clear and consistent process for making major decisions on new products and enhancements.* At the completion of each phase, the PAC determines whether the development efforts should be continued, canceled, or refocused; resolves major issues; changes resource allocation; and so on.
2. *Empower project teams to execute a project plan.* The Phase Review Process enables the PAC to set priorities, approve or revise project direction, set product and project goals, and monitor projects. It can then empower a project team to execute the next phase of the project.
3. *Provide the link for applying product strategy to product development.* Through the Phase Review Process, the PAC can direct development efforts toward overall company strategies.
4. *Provide measurable checkpoints to monitor progress.* The process defines the checkpoints that the PAC can use to review progress on both schedule and product objectives.
5. *Establish milestones that emphasize a sense of urgency.* Phase reviews are intentionally established as milestones at which issues need to be resolved and decisions need to be made. These milestones instill a sense of urgency. A sense of urgency is necessary since most issues get resolved within two weeks of when they need to be resolved, no matter how much time is provided to do it.

Phase Requirements

The specific requirements of each phase vary by company, but we have found a high level of commonality. In the first two phases, the requirements are related more to thorough planning and effective decision making. In later phases, there tends to be some variation based on the characteristics of the product being developed. A summary of the objectives of each phase, along with illustrations of the decisions at the end of the phases, will help to make this clear.

Phase 0 — Concept Evaluation

The objectives of Phase 0 are to enable a company to rapidly evaluate product opportunities and start the product development process as quickly as possible. A product opportunity usually enters this phase through the platform plan or product line plan of the product strategy process. The result of Phase 0 is an evaluation of the concept and opportunity for the product, which is presented to the PAC for Phase I funding, and the outcome of a successful phase review is the assignment of a project team and funding for Phase I.

The primary focus of Phase 0 is to analyze the market opportunity and strategic fit. An example illustrates how this applies. A minicomputer manufacturer formed a team to design the second in a family of new products shortly after the initial product had been released. The team developed the concept for a higher-performance product incorporating additional features and new technology, but at the Phase 0 presentation they were unable to answer the question of why this would be a winning product. The PAC sent them back to answer the question. After four weeks of intense work, during which they contacted a large number of customers, they returned for another Phase 0 review with the answer to the question — a totally different product. What customers really wanted was a lower-cost version of the existing product. Without the Phase Review Process the company would have spent almost $40 million developing the other product and would not have had the resources to develop the product that the market really needed.

An effective Phase 0 review can launch product development efforts in the right direction, even when they start off in the wrong direction. This was the case when one company directed a small group to begin developing scaled-down versions of its existing products in order to open some new market opportunities. The team defined a new product incorporating the most essential features of a recently released product but at 80% of the cost. Although the team was quite enthusiastic about this product, the PAC realized at the Phase 0 review that this product would really just take sales away from the company's existing products and would not open any significant markets. As a result of this realization, they redirected the team to start again and investigate what would be required to open new market opportunities. Without this formal review point, the product would have been well on its way to development before these questions were asked.

During Phase 0, a company evaluates an opportunity, using assumptions — with the assumptions clearly identified and reviewed for validity. This enables a company to take action before a significant investment is made. A communications company benefited from this when it launched a project to develop a product that would get it into an emerging market segment. When the proposed product was reviewed in Phase 0, the PAC realized that the price of the product could be expected to decline below cost as the market emerged, and every unit would be sold at a loss. This was primarily because the new product lacked any unique differentiation from other products already on the market. The PAC canceled the project before significant development funds had been expended. Prior to the new Phase Review Process, the company would have spent eighteen months and $4 million developing the product and then not release it because it would lose money.

Only a few people work on the project during Phase 0. Generally this will include a product champion with the assistance of a few other key individuals. It is expected that the product champion will be encouraged to consult with other experts throughout the company in completing the phase requirements. If properly defined, this phase should be completed in four to eight weeks.

Phase I — Planning and Specification

Phase I is the fundamental building block of the product development effort. The objectives of this phase are to clearly define the product, identify competitive advantages, clarify functionality, determine the feasibility of development, verify to a greater degree of accuracy the estimates made in Phase 0, and plan the development effort for Phase II and the rest of the project. It is important that critical design elements are understood in sufficient detail to analyze their feasibility, but detailed design is not typically done in this phase. At the end of this phase, resource, schedule, and dollar estimates are made for the development of the product; however, funding will only be allocated to complete Phase II.

The Phase I review enables senior management to resolve any remaining issues necessary to make the product development effort successful. For example, the PAC at one company used the Phase I review to resolve some issues for a new high-volume electronic product with innovative performance characteristics. The PAC directed the team to focus more effort on the differentiating features of the product, assigned two additional software engineers in order to accelerate completion by two months, resolved the timing on the international release of the product, and initiated related efforts to improve the integration of this product with other products. Without a review point at which they had to be resolved, these issues would have stretched out indefinitely and slowed the completion of the product.

Phase I reviews also allow senior management to establish priorities among projects and allocate resources accordingly. A computer company launched an effort to develop a new disk storage device that was planned to require five engineers. At the Phase I review several interesting details came to light. First, the disk storage device could only work in conjunction with the next-generation computer being developed, yet would beat the computer to market by over a year. Second, the project was now expected to require eighteen engineers. These engineers would have to be taken off the next-generation computer project, which would further delay its introduction. Finally, the new disk storage device would not be a dramatic improvement over the company's existing product already on the market. The PAC canceled the project and reassigned the engineers to higher-priority programs.

Estimates of factors such as product cost, selling price, quality/reliability measures, projected unit sales, and completion date — that were assumptions in Phase 0 — are analyzed in more detail in Phase I. This was seen in a company developing a new product for a mature market. The product had more features and a lower cost than the company's existing products. During the

Phase 0 review of the product, the PAC considered the cost assumptions to be too high and directed the team to focus on lowering them in Phase I. At the end of Phase I, the team recommended going ahead with the project even though the more accurate estimates showed an even higher cost. The PAC decided, however, that they did not want to invest money in a low-profit product for a mature market and canceled the project.

During Phase I, initial top-level designs may be started. For some product development efforts there may be a choice to be more aggressive and conduct more detailed design, but this should require specific approval at the Phase 0 review.

During Phase I more people are involved in the project effort, and at this point the project takes on a formal team structure, such as a Core Team. Additional resources will also become involved in supporting the efforts. At the end of Phase I, the PAC should decide to either cancel the project or fund the Phase II effort, but it is also possible that the project team will be directed to resolve a specific issue before approval.

Phase II — Development

The objective of Phase II is to develop the product based on the development program approved at the Phase I review, and the majority of the detailed design and development activity takes place during this phase. Before beginning development, the company should conduct formal technical design reviews. During this phase the primary emphasis is on execution rather than analysis of the product opportunity or its feasibility.

The company should initiate manufacturing and support process development concurrently, including manufacturing and test-process development, product-announcement planning, and the customer-service process. Resource requirements significantly increase, and the majority of the development funding will be expended during this phase. Depending on the length of this phase there may be some periodic progress reporting, but if the project team encounters problems that significantly change any of the key factors, such as estimated cost or completion date, it should repeat the Phase I review.

Many milestones and intermediate completions occur during this phase, but the primary objective is usually the completion of a working product. The definition of working can be subjective in some cases, as one company found. At the end of Phase II the product, a high-performance computer, was working but not to expected performance levels. The PAC approved the release to Phase III with a modified approach that would work with selected beta-test customers to identify how to improve performance based on their use of the new system.

Approval from the PAC at the end of Phase II is the judgment that the product is ready for test and evaluation and that the plan for doing this is appropriate. In one project the PAC delayed approval at this stage because the software for the product was not sufficiently completed in order to do the necessary level of testing. The alternative, to initiate testing of the product with incomplete software, was proposed by the project team but rejected by the PAC.

Phase III — Test and Evaluation

The objective of Phase III is to complete acceptance testing and prepare for volume production and product launch. Completion of this phase is marked by a successfully tested product, approved manufacturing and support processes, and a product launch plan.

At the completion of this phase, a Phase III review is held to make the final determination on whether the product is ready for initial shipment. Approval at this point is an approval to manufacture, market, distribute the product, and support it in the field.

One company with a strong commitment to quality uses this phase review as a final checkpoint to ensure that its quality standards are being met. In a fiercely competitive market in which there were already significant orders for a new product, the PAC delayed its final Phase III approval until the product's quality goals had been attained.

Phase IV — Product Release

Phase IV typically includes volume production, product launch marketing, initial distribution, and early support of the product. The Phase IV review is held to verify that these steps have been taken successfully. It also serves as an assessment of early product performance and customer acceptance. Typically it takes place three to six months after initial shipment.

During Phase IV, the product is released to the market. Some remaining tasks may be associated with the initial release of the product, but they should be manageable in order to obtain approval. The remaining work does not include follow-on or enhancement efforts to software or other product options. At the end of this phase, responsibility is passed from the project team to the functional departments to manage the product on an ongoing basis. The project team, however, is responsible for resolving any product problems that occur before the Phase IV review.

The Phase IV review is also a convenient time to review product enhancement, general issues, and recommended process or design changes. It is also an appropriate time for the Core Team to do an assessment of the development process and make recommendations to those responsible for maintaining it. For example, one company that launched a very successful product used this phase review to identify the opportunities to expand the product line based on early customer feedback. As a result, it launched two new projects into a Phase 0.

Why Some Companies Don't Have an Effective Review Process

Some companies mistakenly think that they have a decision-making process similar to a Phase Review Process since they use that name to describe something that they do, but they wonder why they have not achieved much benefit from it. In these cases, we typically find the following underlying causes of failure:

- The process may exist on paper but not be followed. It is seen as a guide-line or suggestion, but when considered to be inconvenient it is ignored.
- The review process may be implemented as a document-based or sign-off process instead of an action-oriented process. It is used to specify the documentation that is necessary at every phase, and the required documentation continually increases. In some cases, the process can significantly increase product development time.
- The review process may be managed by functional organizations. Instead of a cross-functional PAC, department and functional heads must approve projects at the end of each phase. Since they do not convene as a group to make decisions, they circulate approval documents for sign-off. This also slows the development process as changes get made to get approval and documents recirculate for months.
- The cultural change associated with this new form of organization and decision making may not be made. Action-oriented timely decisions by a senior management team may be foreign to the culture of some companies. The necessary cultural change may need some facilitation.
- Phase requirements and expectations may not be clear. Senior management and project teams may have differing expectations. This leads to continued frustration and redirection of project efforts.

References

1. Rick Whiting, "Managing Product Development from the Top," *Electronic Business* (June 17, 1991): 42.
2. For additional information on product development funnels, see Steven C. Wheelwright and Kim B. Clark, *Revolutionizing Product Development* (New York: The Free Press, 1992), 111.

CHAPTER 4

The Core Team Approach to Project Organization

Michael T. Anthony

New products are developed through the coordinated efforts of many people — people who apply different skills and work together on the thousands of tasks needed to create a new product. To work together successfully, they need to co-ordinate their activities, communicate what they are doing, and collectively make decisions. An effective project team organization is necessary to make this happen.

Project organization is one of the most essential elements of product de-velopment, yet few companies have implemented a consistently effective ap-proach to it. Some do not even have a clearly stated way to organize product development projects; they leave it to each team to figure out how to organize. Not having a clearly defined project organization is a little like selecting peo-ple for a football team and then telling them to go out onto the field and play. The players don't know what position to play or how they should play together as a team. They may not even know who should be on the field when or who should do what. It's very difficult for a team to win with this type of confusion.

Still other companies may be able to describe their organizational ap-proach, but they can't get their teams to work effectively, usually because of organizational conflicts and an inconsistent understanding of how the team should work. Some companies continuously experiment with different forms of project organization in hopes of ultimately finding an approach that works. They attempt to improve product development by changing their approach to project organization each time a major crisis occurs.

What separates close-knit teams that work well together, rapidly bring-ing new products to market, from a gathering of functional representatives merely wasting time at weekly meetings? The close-knit teams are effective in communication, coordination, and decision making; these are the primary characteristics of successful teams.

To achieve these characteristics, PRTM developed the Core Team approach to project organization. It enables the quickest time-to-market through efficient coordination and communication, combined with effective decision making. The Core Team approach also provides the basis for true empowerment of the team and the implementation of concurrent engineering activities involved in product development.

Characteristics of a *Successful* Project Team Organization

The secret to successful product development teams lies in organizing them to achieve effective communication, coordination, and decision making. Members of high-performance teams can effectively and efficiently communicate with each other without even realizing that they are doing so. Letting each other know about progress, issues, and key decisions is second nature. Frequently, communication is organic; it just happens naturally as it's supposed to, enabling rapid execution and eliminating mistakes all too common in product development.

Coordinating the numerous activities that must be synchronized is also second nature to successful product development teams. Individual members know which activities must be handled carefully with other members and which can be handled on an individual basis. They know who has responsibility for various activities and when interdependencies need to be managed. Excellent teams are able to manage this coordination efficiently, without extensive meetings, memos, or other non-value-added administrative activities.

Effective decision making is the third characteristic of teams that excel in product development. As a team they know which decisions need to be made and when to make them. The team members understand which decisions are within their span of control and which require the attention of others with a more strategic or technical focus. They make decisions rather than letting things happen by default.

Communication

The high degree of uncertainty and variability involved in product development underscores the importance of good communication. Those working together on the project need to communicate results and identify issues that affect the work of others on the team. Problems need to be communicated to those who can help resolve them. Technical details and specifications need to be communicated to those who use them. Many questions need to be asked and responded to rapidly.

To be effective, communication must take place both vertically — without regard for levels or rank — and horizontally across functional boundaries. Traditional communication through a chain of command can be quite slow and error prone. Obviously, the more people that are involved, the more time is taken to communicate effectively. When communication requires repetition from one person to another, it is subject to delays. Project teams need seamless communication and access to executive management at critical points in the project.

Much of the actual or true information can be lost through organizational filtering. For example, managers may neglect to tell the full story to their director in order to give themselves some time to get the project back on track. The director in turn does more filtering prior to transferring the message to vice presidents, and so on. Soon all this filtering cleans the message to the point that senior managers think that everything on the project is going well. Eventually, they get surprised by an "unexpected" schedule slippage. If everyone had communicated effectively, senior managers might have been able to do something to help the team before the problem got out of hand.

Another reason to ensure quick and effective communication, horizontally across various functions as well as through the hierarchy, is to avoid mistakes in interpretation. The children's game of whispering a message to one person and having that person pass it on only to find out that the original message is completely distorted by the time it gets to the last person takes place routinely in many companies.

Finally, lack of communication has been the cause of many product deficiencies and project delays. The people who needed to communicate didn't. For example, on one project the project manager put together a schedule that assumed one week for tooling. Purchasing knew that a particular part required twelve weeks for tooling, but never saw the schedule to estimate the tooling cycle time. Communication was assumed to have taken place but didn't. The product was four months late, and the broken commitments led to lost customers.

The need for effective communication starts as the product concept evolves into a list of potential features and functions. During this time, frequent, almost constant, communication is needed between marketing and development. Trade-off decisions regarding functionality, the partitioning of features, analysis of what competitors may do, the capabilities of the company, estimates of the market window, and the desires of the marketplace can be achieved only by effective communication within the project team. Rarely does a sequential hand-off from marketing to design engineering to manufacturing work successfully. The organizational structure of the development team can either facilitate easy and effective communication or make communication more difficult.

Some companies try to compensate by imposing extensive written documentation requirements. Development teams can get bogged down with excessive non-value-added tasks, such as preparing status updates, making management presentations, and coordinating formal approval sign-offs. One maker of industrial controllers, for example, had key technical people on the development team spending 30% of their time on activities that did not contribute to the successful completion of the project. These people were giving executive briefings twice a week, making three presentations a week to other functions about the project, and conducting technical demonstrations about their great ideas.

So much time was spent on these tasks not directly related to completing the project that we estimated they could pull in their schedule by six months if they reduced this activity. Since they didn't believe that this was possible, we challenged them to dedicate just one day a week to focus entirely on developing the product. They could do no presentations, hold no meetings, or attend any management update sessions. They could only participate in design and development activity. The results from this minor change were so substantial that the team decided to reduce its non-project activities even more, and as a result got its product to market in record time with a higher quality level than any other project in the company's history.

As the number of people on a given project increases, the number of possible communication paths rises geometrically. For example, a small project with only four individuals involved would have the following twelve communication paths for persons A, B, C, and D:

A→B	B→A	C→A	D→A
A→C	B→C	C→B	D→B
A→D	B→D	C→D	D→C

Product development commonly involves many more people, however. Figure 4–1 depicts the dramatic increase in communication paths $(N \times (N - 1))$ as more people become involved in the project. With sixty people involved in product design, each issue or piece of information can be communicated more than 3,500 ways, and when there are hundreds of these to be communicated each month, it can become quite complex.

Coordination of Activities

Developing new products requires the completion of thousands and sometimes hundreds of thousands of activities; many of these activities are interdependent. Efficient execution of numerous activities requires effective coordination, and as the complexity of the product or its marketing channels increases, the amount of coordination required to manage the project also increases.

Ineffective coordination can lead to project delays and inefficiencies. A multinational instrument company experienced this problem. Because the product development organization was convoluted, most of a project's time-to-market was spent in resource-coordination activities, such as determining which technical experts should jump in to help the team at key points in the

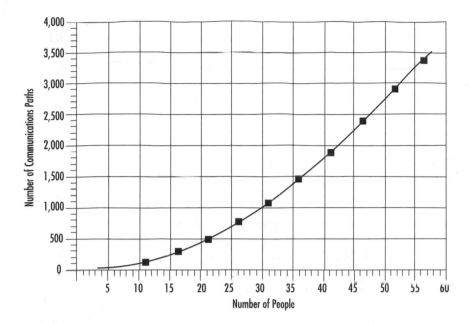

FIGURE 4–1   Communication paths related to number of people on a development team.

process, or backfilling for designers who were pulled to put out fires on other projects.

Ineffective coordination can also cause activities to take place out of sequence. All too frequently engineering begins development before marketing finalizes the product requirements. For example, a company designed and built working prototypes of the six printed circuit boards of a new computer only to find out that they all had to be significantly changed when the product requirements were finalized. Eight man-years of key technical resources were wasted.

Some companies attempt to overcome coordination problems with comprehensive scheduling systems such as detailed Project Evaluation Review Technology (PERT) charts. Usually this requires significant overhead and does not effectively coordinate activities. One company tried to coordinate activities on a complex project by using a PERT chart that covered a 30-foot wall. Two full-time people updated the chart continuously, but on any given day nobody knew what he or she was supposed to do.

Concurrent engineering involves effective coordination of all functions throughout a project, particularly in the early phases. This need for coordination has proven to be a roadblock for many companies that have tried to implement a concurrent engineering approach but can't seem to make it happen. The project team organization doesn't provide the coordination needed.

Successful project teams are able to efficiently coordinate activities with little wasted effort. They know what has to be done and who has to do it. Brief team meetings serve to coordinate upcoming activities, and they use the team organization structure rather than scheduling systems as the primary coordination process.

Decision Making

Developing a new product involves making thousands of decisions. Some are significant, many are small, but all need to be made efficiently. Making the right decisions on a timely basis is another factor that sets apart the successful from the unsuccessful project teams.

Effective project teams make better decisions. Different points of view, skills, and background provide them with synergy in decision making. We illustrate this during our workshops using an exercise called "Lost at Sea." In this exercise, individuals are asked to rank fifteen items that they would take with them if they were set adrift in the middle of the ocean. They then go through the same exercise in small groups. Each set of answers is then scored using U.S. Coast Guard rankings. Inevitably, the scores of the group are higher than the scores of the individuals, demonstrating the power of the team to make better decisions.

Product development decisions also need to be timely. When decisions go unmade for weeks or months, a project can drift and time-to-market lengthens. This has been one of the primary reasons for delays in product development. For example, one company could not decide which microprocessor to use in its product. This was a difficult decision, but it went unresolved for almost eighteen months. After six months, engineers began designing the product without the decision being made. When it was finally made, almost all the work needed to be redone and the product was a year late to market. Without direction, a team will usually do something to keep busy even if it's the wrong thing.

Empowerment of project teams is a popular concept. It gives the team the power to make the decisions when they are needed. Unfortunately, empowerment is frequently stifled because the responsibility and authority of the project team are not clear.

Functional Organization of Product Development

Despite the success of cross-functional project organizations for product development, many companies still organize product development functionally. Under this approach, each function contributes to the product development process in a serial, or hand-off, fashion — similar to a relay race. The development cycle starts with marketing's requirements for the product. These requirements are then handed off to engineering to prepare specifications and begin designing the product. Manufacturing then builds prototypes and pilot units, and sales next fills up the distribution pipeline. Finally, customer service gets involved to support initial sales and handle customer complaints.

The functional approach may lend itself to projects characterized by a defined series of sequences with minimal overlap, but it is generally not well suited to product development. We find that the functional product development approach tends to foster a "throw-it-over-the-wall" attitude, where people wash their hands of responsibility and accountability for the project once they complete their particular tasks. Many times this flaw is hidden because the organization is too busy to go back and compare the actual performance of the entire project to the original objectives.

Another drawback to a functional product development approach is that it usually creates a cumbersome system of sign-offs and approvals in which there are constant hand-offs and hand-backs. This time-consuming system typically arises from problems that occurred in the past. Once the problem is fixed, someone decides that avoiding it in the future requires a formal sign-off, at which each function must review and approve the product before proceeding. That way there is an audit trail that can be reviewed in order to identify who is to blame. After a while the problems no longer occur, but layers of sign-offs have accumulated and development time has been extended.

For example, a manufacturer of electronic instruments overran its budget for prototype materials by $860. Management countered by establishing a procedure that required four vice presidents to sign off on all prototype material procurement for a new product. The resulting time spent chasing these executives for their signatures greatly escalated development costs and needlessly lengthened time-to-market.

A functional structure has many vertical layers and generally lacks the horizontal network necessary for effective communication and coordination and rapid decision making that characterize successful product development. This can create functional gridlock, which stalls new product decisions. For example, if manufacturing does not order materials for a prototype unit until the designs are formally approved, structural delays creep in between the sequential steps. What starts out as a system with control points often becomes a bureaucratic maze that people circumvent instead of taking the time to fix. These are typical symptoms of companies that have longer product development cycles.

Figure 4–2 illustrates the confusing communication tangle of the functional organization approach. To develop new products under the functional approach, information must move horizontally across the various functions, as well as vertically through many levels in the organization. The number of communication paths quickly increases, and each communication path adds to total cycle time.

When the functional approach works well, it's merely slow; when it works poorly, very few new products come out in time to be competitive. When conflict arises, issues get bumped up to the next level for resolution. Eventually,

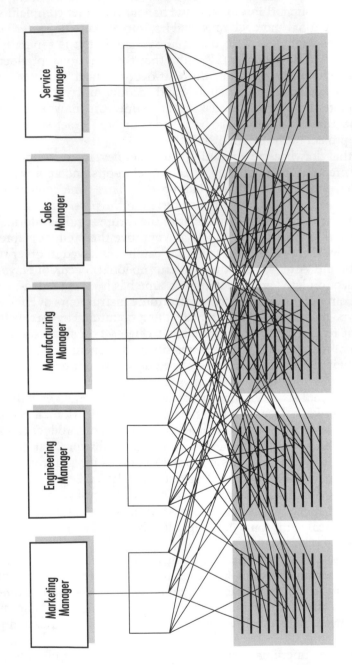

FIGURE 4–2   Functional organization, showing the interfunctional communication tangle.

product decisions are made by those with the loudest voice or the most political clout, instead of the people closest to the design and the customer.

The primary defect of the functional approach lies in the structure itself. The performance of people within any given function is measured and rewarded according to that function's goals and objectives. As a result, those involved in product development tend to strive for functional excellence. Often what is best for the individual functional organization, however, may not be good for the product or company as a whole. Functional goals may not always be consistent with company goals, and they are frequently inconsistent with the goals of other functions.

Project teams at a minicomputer company were functionally organized, with marketing and sales, R&D, engineering, advanced manufacturing, manufacturing, and customer service. Each of these functions was involved in the new product development process at different points. Marketing usually initiated development with a list of requirements that it thought a new product should have. Marketing passed a marketing requirements document (MRD) to the engineering organization. Engineering consequently would start with the MRD and decide what it would and would not do. A product functional specification (PFS) would then describe what engineering would design. Unfortunately, the MRD and PFS typically were not aligned.

Manufacturing became involved in the project only when it came time to build pilot units. Since the engineers ordered all the parts and built their own prototypes, manufacturing had to start from scratch. Much time was spent trying to understand the design and to find standard, acceptable components. Finally, just before the first customer shipment, customer service found out about the project. Of course, it needed to have spare parts strategically located around the country. This meant that manufacturing had to ramp up even faster and that engineers had to stabilize the growing number of engineering changes quickly.

As a result of this functional orientation, the company took twice as long to develop new products as its competitors. Eventually it was sold to a foreign company, which attempted to make improvements only to be frustrated by the strong functional mentality.

While individuals within disparate functions often know their profession well, they may not understand what is important to other functional groups. Figure 4–3 illustrates that what one functional expert finds rewarding and interesting frequently has no bearing on the interests of experts from other functions. Each step that one works on individually is shaded by one's own specialized interests. This bias shapes the product in ways that detract from its success.

At a computer manufacturer, marketing specified that a new computer should be able to meet all the needs of a wide variety of industry and military applications. Engineering added the specification that it have the most advanced processor technology that would be available in a year. Although these extremes were not necessary, the product was defined to include them. After a

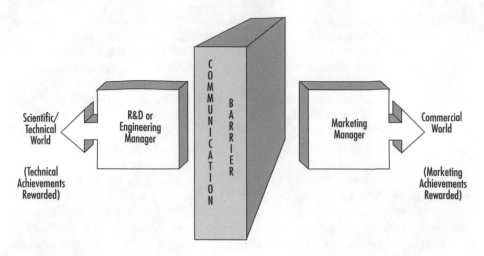

FIGURE 4–3   Functional organization breeds barriers (people remain isolated within their field of expertise).

year, the company realized that the product would cost too much and take too long to develop. It was redefined to focus on real needs.

The functional organization structure for product development works well in small, closely knit companies with limited product variability. In these firms, everyone knows everyone else and generally they all have ample experience working together. Start-up companies exemplify this and are frequently used as models of how this approach works. When a small company is developing a single product, however, the entire company is essentially a project team.

Some large companies try to mimic a small company organization in order to achieve efficient communication, coordination, and decision making. They form smaller autonomous business units with profit-and-loss responsibility and control over their own resources. While this does achieve some of these advantages within the business unit, it makes interaction outside of the business unit even more difficult. As a result, the company sacrifices the use of common resources and other economies of scale that provide an advantage to larger companies. The Core Team approach strikes a better balance.

The Core Team Approach

When we first started working with our clients to improve the product development process, we developed the Core Team approach as an alternative for organizing product development teams. After applying the Core Team concept repeatedly with exceptional results, we realized that it was a superior way of organizing, directing, and managing project teams. We now believe that it is the best form of project organization for product development.

While the Core Team generally consists of five to eight individuals with different skills and a Core Team leader, it does not use the classical hierarchical approach to organization. All product development responsibilities are divided among the team members, and individual team members' responsibilities are usually associated with their skills. Recognizing the need to move away from vertical hierarchies, strict functional representation, and pay-grade-level politics, we believed that the Core Team structure had to be represented by a continuous circle. As the circle implies, all team members are equals. No single function has more status than another.

The circle also suggests that everyone faces the same challenge: to do what it takes to get the right product out to the customer quickly. This implies completing tasks that may be outside team members' strict functional areas or below what would normally be considered their stature.

Individual team members focus less on representing a function and more on carrying out the tasks that contribute to the ultimate success of the project. They do not operate within the normal constraints of job descriptions; they are more flexible and work as a team to do what needs to be done. Core Team members execute their responsibilities directly, on their own, by supervising people assigned to them and by coordinating with functional specialists.

The Core Team approach differs from other forms of project organization in that the Core Team is directly responsible for the project's success. In the functional organization, responsibility is imposed, while with the Core Team structure, accountability is accepted. In a hierarchical structure, detailed decisions are generally made or approved at higher organizational levels, but in the Core Team organization, decisions are made closest to the point of action, by the people most familiar with the problem. To help them make the best decisions, Core Teams get advice, counsel, and guidance from functional specialists.

A Core Team organization consists of four main elements: a Core Team leader, the Core Team, the full project team, and a Core Team facilitator. These are illustrated in Figure 4–4.

Core Team Leader

At the center of the Core Team is the Core Team leader. This individual has the responsibility and accountability for ensuring that the product meets its goals for time-to-market, quality, development expense, and product cost. The Core Team leader is the hub of the team. The role of a Core Team leader varies in a subtle but significant way from that of a project manager in a matrix organization. The Core Team leader is more of a team captain than part-time boss. The emphasis is on leadership, not dictatorship. This person acts as the quarterback (in the American football analogy), leading and motivating the team to achieve the design and project goals.

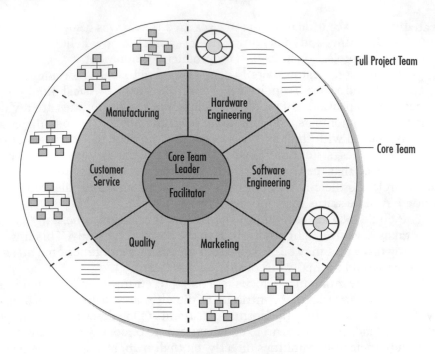

FIGURE 4–4   Basic Core Team structure.

The Core Team leader is also responsible for managing the project budget, resources, and schedule. The Core Team leader works to resolve conflicts among Core Team members, and when conflicts or issues arise between Core Team members and people in functional organizations, the Core Team leader helps to bring about resolution.

Good Core Team leaders do not make unreasonable demands on their team. On the contrary, the best Core Team leaders have excellent interpersonal skills. A telecommunications company once made an experienced product manager the Core Team leader for an important new product, but this person didn't fully understand the role. He constantly alienated the engineering and manufacturing Core Team members by pounding his fist on the table and screaming that they were missing their schedules and budgets. This had the opposite effect from motivating the team to get the project on track.

Core Team Members

The Core Team members surround the Core Team leader. The specific makeup of the Core Team will vary based on the product being developed, its complexity, and its market. For smaller, simpler projects, the Core Team could consist of as few as four or five people. On complex projects, a somewhat larger Core Team can manage many people. For example, one very large project had

1,800 people managed by a Core Team of ten people. In any case, a Core Team should almost always include members from engineering, manufacturing, marketing, and customer service.

Core Team members coordinate project activities for their particular functions. They act as conduits (see Figure 4–5) for communicating both functional needs into the development effort and project requirements back into the functional organization. This ensures a product that is manufacturable, serviceable, and meets customer requirements.

Core Team members also manage the project resources for the activities for which they have responsibility. For example, the electronic engineering Core Team member in a data communications development team manages engineers working on processor, communication, and interface boards, as well as those working on backplanes and power systems. These individuals are members of the full project team. Members of the full project team work on the product at specific points in the process. Full project team members come into and exit the project as their work is completed. The responsible Core Team members contribute to the performance evaluation of their full project team members.

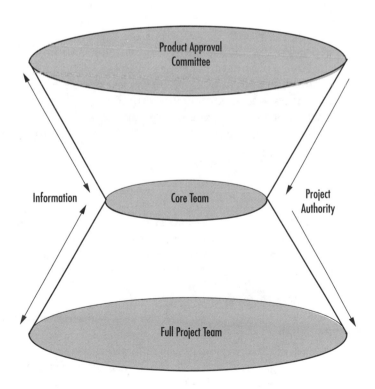

FIGURE 4–5   Core Team as information conduit.

One U.S. consumer electronics company no longer has a quality function represented on the Core Team. This company has achieved so much in the way of improving quality that it is an integral part of every person's job. Quality needs no representation because it is already embedded in the team.

Full Project Team

The next layer out from the Core Team, the full project team comprises the individual contributors from various functions that are involved in a portion of the project managed by a specific Core Team member. Members of the full project team can be assigned directly to the project or are functional managers who are involved in supporting new products.

Those assigned directly are typically product development engineers, technicians, and specialists who complete various project tasks. For example, ten software engineers can be assigned to software development. Full project team members can be assigned permanently or temporarily, and full-time or part-time. Their work is coordinated by a designated Core Team member.

Functional managers and other experts may participate as part of the full team to coordinate specific activities. For example, a component engineer and purchasing manager may be involved in the qualification of a new supplier.

Core Team members frequently have members on the full project team who are not resident in their own functional organization. For example, a hardware Core Team member often has full project team members from CAD (computer-aided design), regulatory, component engineering, procurement, and manufacturing engineering functional organizations.

Full project team members work on the project either full-time or part-time, depending on the scope and intensity of their work. They typically come into the project when needed. It is the responsibility of the Core Team member to negotiate with various functional managers for the time needed. Core Team members typically will provide input to the performance evaluations of individuals working on their full project teams.

Facilitators

Facilitators are charged with helping Core Team leaders and members through the development process. They have a process improvement focus versus a project focus. Many people think of them as an on-line help system to guide the Core Team through the steps in the development process and through initial phase reviews.

Facilitators help Core Teams utilize the product development process to achieve the best possible results. They are process engineers who understand how to get things done.[1] They also frequently assist the Core Team leader in planning, scheduling, and coordinating project activities.

Additionally, facilitators measure the development process, monitor trends, plan improvements, and implement new tools. Their responsibility is to be the manager of the product development *process* and assist in implementing it across all projects.

Functional Managers

At first many functional managers are uncomfortable with the implementation of the Core Team structure in the organization. They question their own role in an organization where the Core Team will make all project-level decisions.

In reality, it is impossible for functional managers to contribute to more than one or two projects and still maintain their functional responsibilities. Some try to implement elaborate progress reporting; others use weekly briefings. While this may help them to understand project status, it does not enable them to contribute to the project's progress. The result is excessive overhead, built-in decision-making delays, and confusion over who is really responsible.

The Core Team structure eliminates the demands on functional management for day-to-day implementation-level details of product development. Functional managers can then concentrate on functional excellence, advancing the technical knowledge of their organization, setting long-term plans and strategy, and allocating resources across multiple Core Teams. They become more efficient and are also able to better leverage their experience.

For a functional manager, moving to the Core Team structure can be somewhat threatening. It's not very comfortable knowing that people who in the past needed approval of every decision will now be making implementation-level decisions on their own or with their fellow Core Team members. Typically this requires a transition period, since individuals will be new to the Core Team member role and not confident in their ability to make decisions. Functional managers likewise also need to see a track record of successful decision making before they are willing to relinquish control.

Time-to-Market and Project Organization

Figure 4–6 illustrates how time-to-market is directly affected by the way a project team is organized. The upper horizontal axis shows an approach to resource participation that ranges from staff-assigned task responsibility to resources dedicated to a project team. The amount of coordination and communication required to develop the product is also plotted horizontally, on the lower horizontal axis. Generally, less coordination and communication is required as project participation moves toward more dedicated resources.

On the vertical axis, project management approaches range from essentially no management to a single project manager who is in charge from start to finish, with many variations in between. Also on the vertical axis is the time required for decision making. This goes from slow to rapid as more

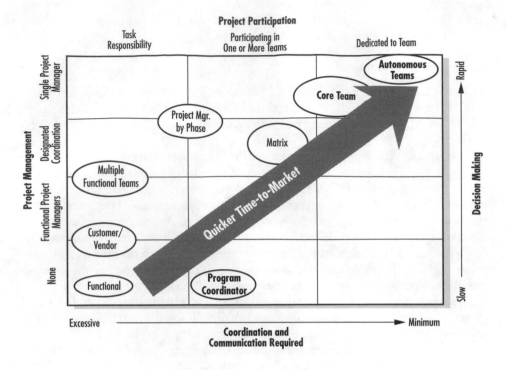

FIGURE 4–6   Time-to-market and project organization.

focused project management greatly reduces the amount of time required to make decisions.

Seven different forms of project organization, including Core Teams, are positioned on this chart to illustrate the performance differences of the various approaches. Those positioned up and to the right have more efficient coordination and communication as well as efficient decision making. The Core Team and autonomous team organizations have the highest performance, but the autonomous team is so extreme that it sacrifices any functional involvement.

A company making telecommunications products was able to increase project effectiveness by changing its approach to project organization. Traditionally, it had specific functional task teams or experts that participated in sub-elements of a given product's design. These sub-elements were optimized by each task team; however, no one took an overall product viewpoint. The company spent weeks making the simplest decisions because many people participated in the project, each having his or her own view of what was right. Coordination was done by a large staff function called project administration. It was this group's charter to attempt to coordinate a high level of activity across many individuals. Communication went up vertically in the functional organization, then horizontally across functions, and then down again.

Dedicating project resources for major projects and selecting a single project manager from specification through to volume manufacturing acceptance helped to greatly reduce this company's time-to-market. Projects that had taken fifty months in the past now took thirty months to complete. Decisions were more timely. Coordination and communication became more efficient. By making these improvements, the company was able to move from the lower left-hand sector of the chart in Figure 4–6 to the upper right-hand sector. They moved along the diagonal that improves time-to-market.

Empowerment

Empowerment involves giving a group the responsibility and authority to do a specific job. It is a powerful concept, but it is often misapplied. One product development consultant claimed that the true test of empowerment is "when a project team can develop any product they want and they are not restricted by company policies requiring approval for things like hiring, capital spending, etc." This is the wrong interpretation of empowerment.

Meeting common goals and objectives is easily facilitated by giving Core Team members the authority and accountability for the project's success. This authority and accountability come from empowering the Core Team with finite, measurable milestones of performance and the resources for development.

PACE enables effective empowerment by establishing a two-layer organization with executive management (the Product Approval Committee, or PAC) and the people directly involved in developing a new product (the Core Team). For improving functional excellence and non-project issues, Core Team members report to and are evaluated by their functional managers. For product development issues, Core Team members are evaluated by the Core Team leader, who in turn is evaluated by the PAC. The PAC empowers the Core Team by allocating resources at each phase of the project and giving the Core Team authority for all implementation-level decisions.

When Core Teams are empowered to make implementation-level decisions in product development, decision making becomes quicker and more effective. Everyone understands who makes what decisions, and these decisions get communicated to those who need to know.

With the Core Team approach, senior management makes the critical strategic decisions regarding the product, but the Core Team members make all of the implementation or tactical decisions necessary to develop the product. This provides two important benefits to the company:

1. Executive time is spent providing strategic direction and control instead of micromanaging lower-level decisions or resolving arguments among functional departments.
2. Most of the project-related decisions are made by the Core Team, which is closest to the project. Because they live and breathe the project every day, these people have the necessary information to make decisions.

The benefits of Core Team empowerment became clear to a vice president of a major computer company who loved to make every major product decision for his 300-person organization. Managers were constantly hounding him, however, to make strategic technical decisions. Once the company established the Core Team structure, this vice president was freed up to focus on the future growth and direction of engineering. Equally important, people developing products learned again how to make good development decisions.

Implementing Concurrent Engineering

Concurrent engineering means developing the product and all of its associated processes (manufacturing, service, distribution) at the same time. The Core Team structure allows a company to implement concurrent engineering. It brings the proper functions into the development project at the correct time. With the Core Team in place, companies develop not only the product but its associated manufacturing, distribution, and service and support processes as well. The objective is to have everything in place before the product hits the market. If process considerations are dealt with during design, time-to-market is generally shorter. Concurrent engineering typically lowers overall product cost because manufacturing and other processes are optimized.

By implementing the Core Team structure and allowing concurrent engineering to really take hold, a company can induce the functions to become stronger as they focus on what they can contribute to new product development. Their task is not to optimize their functional department for the purposes of creating an empire but to properly staff and support ongoing operations as well as product development.

Figure 4–7, which is based on a PRTM survey, illustrates when and to what degree best-practice companies involve the various functions in product development. On the vertical axis, various functional organizations and groups involved in new product development are listed. Across the top of the chart, the phases in the process from concept to volume manufacturing stability are shown. The shading indicates the level of involvement each function has at the various points in the process.

Research is involved heavily up front to transfer technology from the lab, then moves to a monitoring mode. Engineering is involved heavily throughout development, including the hand-off to manufacturing. Manufacturing has substantial involvement early in development, thus designing in manufacturability instead of scrambling late in development. Marketing does not just kick off development but is involved throughout to handle trade-off decisions and prepare for market introduction. Sales is kept informed of the upcoming product and gets involved during testing for sales training and preparation for launch. Quality plays an active role throughout for both product and process design. Service is involved moderately so that serviceability issues are addressed. Finance monitors development throughout to ensure that the project

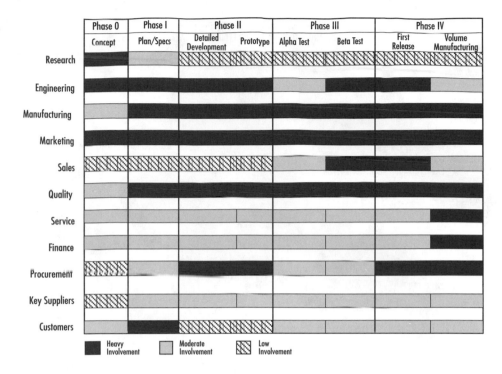

FIGURE 4-7   Concurrent engineering integrates all functions during the development process.

is financially justified and on track in terms of budget. Procurement and key suppliers are involved from specification onward so that all parts and sub-assemblies can be easily integrated and fully utilized. Finally, the product's concept and specifications, as well as test units, are validated with customers.

By using the Core Team organization structure to implement concurrent engineering, companies can also break the project revision cycle (see Figure 4-8). The project revision cycle starts when problems occur during the project that could have been avoided or managed better if the Core Team approach had been used to implement concurrent engineering. These problems, usually in the crisis stage, cause changes in the project. Sometimes the scope or functionality of the product has to be changed; sometimes a change in team members or team leader is needed. Altering the project in these ways delays development as people regroup and replan their efforts.

The vicious part of the cycle occurs when as a result of longer development time, the market shifts towards another approach and the company must again struggle just to catch up. An even worse scenario occurs if a shift in technology takes place.

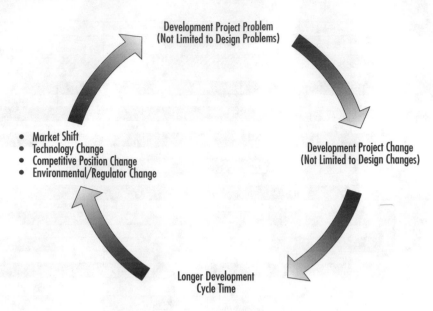

Development Project Problem
(Not Limited to Design Problems)

Development Project Change
(Not Limited to Design Changes)

- Market Shift
- Technology Change
- Competitive Position Change
- Environmental/Regulator Change

Longer Development
Cycle Time

FIGURE 4–8   The project revision cycle.

One manufacturer of thermally activated power switches lost the project revision cycle game. The firm was so caught up in changes to its new product under development that its projected completion date continuously slipped: first three months, then six months, then finally an entire year. In the meantime, a competitor was working on a new switch technology that cost 90% less. As a result, the company caught up in the project revision cycle had to permanently close its doors, eliminating 260 jobs.

Why Some Companies Haven't Been Successful Using Cross-Functional Project Teams

Recently the use of cross-functional teams has become popular. Yet while some companies achieve significant improvements in performance, others don't see any changes. It is simply not enough to put people from multiple functions on a team. We typically find other necessary factors lacking:

- The authorities and responsibilities are not clearly defined between functional departments and project teams.
- The roles and responsibilities of team members are not clear.
- Team leaders are not effective in leading cross-functional teams.

- Teams are not appropriately empowered to do what they need to do. Typically there is no process for empowering them.
- Team members are not sufficiently dedicated to their team responsibilities.
- The teams exist only on paper and do not effectively manage the successful execution of development projects.

References

1. Michael T. Anthony, "PDP Engineer: Career for the '90s?," *The Professional Careers*, Time-to-Market News.

CHAPTER 5

Structured Product Development

Michael T. Anthony

Product development is complex. Developers need to complete thousands, sometimes tens of thousands, of activities. Most of these activities are interdependent, and coordination is complicated. To manage this complexity, the product development process must be properly structured and clearly defined.

By structured, we mean having a framework for the interrelationship of these activities and the principle of organization supporting it, such as a hierarchical structure that is simpler at the top and more detailed at the bottom. By defined, we mean that each activity is distinctly specified. All the people involved in product development know what the activity involves and they do it in the same way.

As simple as this is, it's surprising how many companies can't seem to get it right. In some companies, the product development process is still unstructured and most of the activities are undefined. There is little consistent terminology; each project team uniquely defines its own activities, even though many are similar to those in other projects. As a result, project schedules are not comparable — some define twenty tasks while others define 1,000. There is no way to consistently measure progress, and standard cycle-time estimates cannot be used for scheduling. It's very difficult for those who try to support multiple projects. Without a common structure, the product development process cannot be easily improved.

Other companies have moved in the opposite direction and defined their product development process in detail — too much detail. They try to control every detail by defining how each activity should be done and what the output should look like. Typically this approach is document-based; completion of each task is controlled by preparation and approval of a specifically defined document. This bureaucratic approach to control is frequently established by issuing a thick notebook of rules and regulations with detailed checklists on how things should be done. Fortunately, in most cases these are ignored. Following them would require a project team to take twice as long to develop a product.

Often, companies overlook the need for structure in their rush for defining the product development process. In other cases, the structure itself is not appropriate. Either the levels are not correct or the tasks are misplaced; usually too much information is required too soon.

Structured product development in PACE strikes a balance between discipline and creativity. A well-thought-out process doesn't hinder creativity; it allows development teams to focus on the real issue — developing the product itself — not on reinventing the development process each time.

In PACE, development activities are structured in a hierarchy, from phases (the highest and broadest level), to steps, to tasks, and finally to activities (the most specific). Phases are the same for all projects. As was explained in Chapter 3, this is the primary decision-making level. Steps are the same for all projects (although some projects may omit some). This is the primary level for planning and scheduling. Tasks provide guidelines on how a step can be completed. The Core Team can follow these as appropriate. Activities are left completely to the Core Teams to specify. Collectively, they form the basis for decision making, project scheduling, resource planning, process measurement, and continuous improvement.

The Need for Structure and Definition in the Development Process

Because many companies don't think of new product development as a process, they have never defined the activities required to develop a new product. Even basic terminology is undefined. For example, each project includes a functional-description document. The definition of this should be clear to everyone involved in the project. It should not be thought of as a ten-page summary by one engineer, a sixty-page document by another, and a four hundred-page document by a third.

Lack of consistent terminology wastes enormous time and effort, as those using a vague process try to make sense of it. Typically, extensive and unproductive meetings may be needed just to understand what is going on. Much of this wasted time is due to the lack of structure.

In one case, a data communications company without a structured process seemed to have twice the development resources it required for the amount of development activity under way. Upon investigation, we found that only 30% of people's time was actually spent on designing the product. The other 70% was wasted clearing up misconceptions about what was being done and by whom. Terminology was so inconsistent that product specifications had four different names and twice as many definitions.

We surveyed hundreds of people involved in product development at many companies spanning a broad range of industries, and we inquired how they could benefit by structuring their development process. The results are quite interesting:

1. Hand-offs between groups were misunderstood and often fumbled:
   - Fully 39% of the hand-offs received were garbled or confused, causing wasted effort, misdirected work, and so on. This means that if a project has three hand-offs, at least one is guaranteed to be messed up.
   - Interestingly, 22% of work was knowingly passed on garbled or confused. The many reasons for this included inadequate planning, rushed execution, and lax discipline.

While this was disturbing enough, 39% of work was received garbled or confused. How did the level increase from 22% to 39% (a 17% discrepancy, which is almost double the original 22% level) in the transition? The relationships are fundamentally misunderstood between different groups in the development process. In other words, downstream groups' needs are not understood or appreciated by upstream groups. For example, the CAD (computer-aided design) group may not know what specific information and format manufacturing needs for the bill of materials and thus messes up the hand-off.

2. Fully 42% of work was repeated because of an upstream change such as late customer input, specifications in error, or something being overlooked. This means that two out of every five working days were wasted! If repeat work were eliminated, the productivity of the development organization would increase by 72% (58% good work to 100% good work) without adding any people!

3. At least 48% of development work was fire fighting — unplanned work that pops up unexpectedly and must be dealt with immediately. Fire-fighting solutions are primarily Band-Aid solutions due to time pressures, limited resources, and limited alternatives, because much of the design is already locked in. Fire-fighting work is hastily done and usually fraught with errors.

4. A full 48% of plans created by individuals involved in development was questioned, ignored, or otherwise discredited by managers or peer groups. Since product development is an inherently complex and multifunction process, the overall project schedule is based on the integration of many lower-level schedules. Yet one out of every two schedules was rejected. Why was this? Probably because early schedules are only 45% accurate! Since early schedules tend to be inaccurate, no one believes them. Management then issues unreasonable demands, and the development team responds by padding the schedule.

5. Amazingly, only 28% of development work was truly new. This means that 72% of the work was familiar. If this is so, then why did the problems just described occur? Because there was no process structure and lessons were not learned. Structuring the development process focuses on the 72% of work that has been done before — the mundane blocking and tackling that so often bogs down projects. With this work structured, development teams can focus their energies on the 28% of work that is truly new and innovative, which subsequently adds the most value.

These survey results show the tremendous opportunity that structuring the development process presents.

Concerns Regarding Development Process Structure

Innovation and creativity cannot be precisely planned and controlled, but structuring the routine activities makes possible a focus on the more creative aspects of product development. Traditionally there have been some concerns regarding structuring the development process in technology-driven organizations. Many people treat product development as a creative process. Indeed, portions of product development require some creativity. Once creative people understand that structure, at the appropriate levels, can actually free them of the mundane and boring tasks, they will have more time to spend on the creative, value-added elements. For example, rather than take time to determine the outline and format of a functional specification, engineers can better use their time applying a standard format and defining the product.

Many people feel that structure confines. They complain that it's too rigid and limits flexibility. We agree. The wrong level of structure results in extensive paperwork and bureaucracy. It's finding the right level of structure for the type of product that is important.

When working initially with a client, we sometimes hear that "structured development processes won't work here because we never do the same type of project twice." This is almost never true. Even widely disparate projects have much in common.

Moreover, if product development is approached differently each time, two things happen. First, there is no repeatable learning-curve benefit, so cycle times gradually get longer as projects grow more ambitious. Second, when someone does come up with an improved method or technique, it is not standardized and used by other projects. If steps in the development process are not approached in the same manner each time, it is very difficult to measure the process and improve it.

Many technical people are uncomfortable with structure. They worry about being confined and losing flexibility and creativity. Yet when product development activities are truly understood, it's easy to see that most of them are not new. As was illustrated in the survey just described, the majority of product development tasks are not truly new. By structuring the repetitive tasks, technical experts can concentrate more on what is truly new and unique.

For example, one company in the advanced systems market had a senior technical person who refused to believe that product development could ever be structured. When probed about the new design she was working on, she initially said it was "all new." Upon further investigation, we discovered that, in a hardware sense, only two of the 56 circuit boards were new. Then, after looking closely at each of these, she determined that only four ASICs (application-specific integrated circuits) and some supporting logic were new.

Still another company designing early warning systems for major defense contractors fell into the trap of using its wide product variety and low production volume as excuses for cost overruns and missed schedules. The company believed that this cycle couldn't be reversed because each project was different. Once it understood that although projects may be different, they have common process elements, the company was able to structure its process to be more competitive.

Symptoms of the Need for More Structure

There are many indications that a company needs more structure.

Inconsistent terminology and definitions

Every company has its own product development language. Unfortunately, all too often this language is similar to the Tower of Babel — everyone speaks in a different way, assuming that everyone else understands it in the same way. With terminology that is inconsistent from project to project, people don't understand the context and scope of what has to be done. One company had ten different names for the same market-assessment document. Each version was slightly different, but those differences became more blurred over time. Eventually, no one was certain what the document was supposed to contain. This confusion leads to much non-value-added activity devoted to understanding what people truly mean when they use a term or say they are going to complete a task.

Inaccurate schedules

Product development schedules are only as good as the accuracy of the steps that make them up. If the steps are not clearly understood, then it's difficult to estimate how long they will take. If they are inconsistently defined, then it is impossible to use past experience as a reference point. Inaccurate schedules frequently result from an unstructured process because people are scheduling on assumptions that may not be shared or understood by others in the organization. Nonexistent schedules are an extreme version of inaccurate schedules.

Inability to estimate resource requirements

Resource requirement estimates are only as accurate as estimates of the time taken to complete each step. Without a good, consistent definition of each step, it is impossible to make reasonable estimates. When the estimates are inaccurate, companies are continually late with new products and projects are under- or over-resourced. Structure helps by first defining what has to be done and how long it will take. Once this is understood, the ability to accurately estimate resource requirements greatly improves.

Plans made disjointedly between groups

Without structure, there is little basis for making critical decisions. Plans made by one functional organization don't tie into what other organizations are doing. This results in key activities falling through the cracks. In an electronic systems company that suffered from lack of structure, there was no consistent framework, terminology, or definitions. Consequently, management frequently got lost in the details. Each project manager presented different formats, processes, and levels of detail. Executive managers often weren't able to see the forest for the trees. They grasped at points that were not important and had to make decisions with an unclear picture of how it all tied together. Without structure, coordinating plans made between groups is virtually impossible, since everyone has a different understanding of what must happen.

Excessive task interdependence

Excessive task interdependence occurs when tasks in the development process are delayed or waiting in queue for another task to be completed. An unstructured or poorly structured process is full of this sort of wasted time. Clarifying process tasks and defining what is required for each one greatly reduces task interdependence so that low-cost activities don't slow down or hold up high-cost activities.

Poor understanding of responsibilities

Poor structure results in not knowing who or what group is responsible for the completion of specific activities. PRTM often works in organizations in which the responsibility for critical tasks is not well understood. We have seen fully staffed departments where no one else in the organization knows exactly what the department is doing. This is a key indicator that the development process is confused and roles and responsibilities for the activities are not clearly defined.

Attention focused on fire fighting

Excessive fire fighting is symptomatic of companies with insufficient product development structure. A computer company that we worked with was stuck with a fire-fighting dilemma where executive managers loved to jump in, roll up their sleeves, and help solve problems. They were more comfortable jumping from crisis to crisis than in setting strategy and objectives for everyone else. This came to a head when the executives asked a project team to give them two one-hour updates every day, at 8:00 A.M. and again at 5:00 P.M. The team, of course, spent an hour preparing for each status update and lost four hours of productive work time every day.

No "one way" of developing a product

A company in the electronic imaging business had no consistency from project to project. The steps followed to develop a new product occurred at different places and times for each project. Many of the activities had varying nomenclature, making it difficult for people who had worked many years in the division to interpret what was happening. As a result, no one took advantage of good methods when they were developed.

Too many clarification meetings

Poor process structure leads to a multitude of meetings for clarification purposes. Because next steps are vague, these meetings are required to figure out what has been accomplished, what must be worked on next, and who is to do it. Too many meetings is a sign of a poor process structure.

Large middle-management ranks

The need for structuring new product development is evident when management has to make decisions. Understanding how each project fits in the overall product line plan, its integration with the R&D or technology strategy, and its financial justification can be greatly simplified by a structured process. Without structure, more middle management is required to handle the confusion. Companies that have the correct level of structure have fewer middle management people, since they are not needed for controlling the process.

Time wasted on non-value-added activities

Extensive non-value-added activity can be incurred in order to clarify terminology and intent. The magnitude of this can be enormous. Without structure, more time is spent coordinating activity and redoing tasks because of miscommunication.

A systems company that structured its development process eliminated the white spaces in the process. (White space is time spent during which no value is being added to the project.) This company consequently cut 23% from the cycle time for new products. According to the vice president of engineering, "The real value of this was that we can now use that time and those resources elsewhere, giving us the freedom to work on more new products."

How Much Is Enough?

Companies typically are at either end of the spectrum when it comes to structuring and defining new product development (see Figure 5–1). With an unstructured and undefined process, development activity is usually quite frenetic.

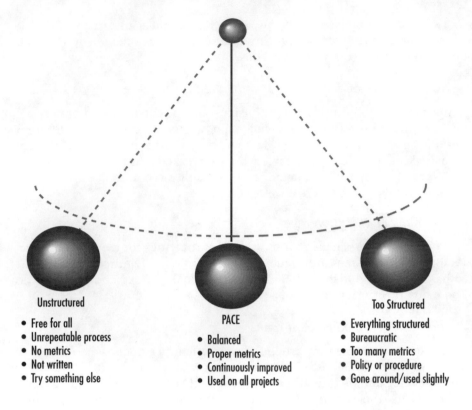

FIGURE 5–1   Range of process structure.

Everyone is running around, no one has time to think, and people really can't see how their pieces of a project fit into the bigger picture. Typically, little is written down, and senior management has to spend most of its time fighting project-related fires.

At the other extreme, companies that have a process that is too structured typically have two systems in place. The first is represented by the five-pound development notebook on everyone's shelf that management thinks is being used. The second is the true process that people follow because the five-pound process is too bureaucratic and slow. These organizations may have done some excellent work in defining many of the details of the product development process, but because it is overly structured and too defined, everything is ignored.

The correct level of structure balances the need for a repeatable, measurable process with the requirement to remain flexible and open to new ideas or approaches. By providing structure at the proper levels and defining steps at the correct time in the development process, PACE achieves this balance so that the development process is used, measured properly, and continually improved.

Levels of Structured Development

Structured product development is a hierarchical blueprint of the product development process that is consistently applied to all product development projects. Within PACE there are four levels of structured development; each level is an aggregate summary of the previous level.

Hierarchical Structure

Structured development under PACE consists of four hierarchical levels: phases, steps, tasks, and activities. Figure 5–2 graphically depicts these levels. As can be seen in this chart, there are typically three to six phases, multiple steps within phases, multiple tasks in each step, and multiple activities in each task.

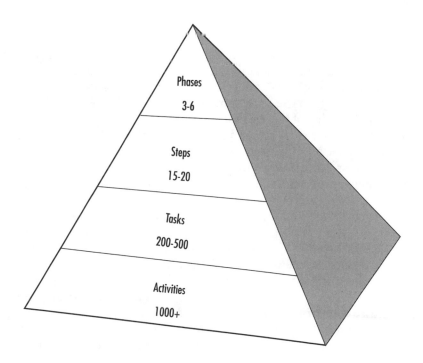

FIGURE 5–2   Levels of structure.

At the highest level of structure are phases. As described in Chapter 3, there are usually three to six phases. Phase end points are milestones in the development process at which decisions are required for funding the next phase. Each phase consists of a number of specific steps.

Steps are the most significant level within structured development. They are used to schedule and manage the progress of development activities. Most companies have fifteen to twenty steps in their development process. Steps are consistently applied to all projects, although some projects may not include all the steps. A software development step, for example, would be the same in all projects, but projects without any software development would omit that step.

Steps consist of multiple tasks, typically twelve to thirty-five tasks for each step. Generally, tasks are consistent from project to project unless there is a significant reason to change them. Tasks are used to compute standard cycle times and define the work to be done. Task completion is the responsibility of the Core Team member in charge of a specific step.

Tasks are broken into a number of activities. These activities can number from several to more than a hundred per task. They are the things that every project team member is doing on a day-to-day basis. Unlike tasks, activities tend to vary based on individual projects, since the actual work may be divided differently from project to project.

Project Overview

Structuring the development process at a high level starts by creating a one-page overview of the entire development process, from concept to volume manufacturing. This high-level overview outlines the phases of development, defines the major steps in the development process, and shows the parallelism, precedence, and overlap of the various steps.

Under PACE, the steps in product development are defined as part of a generic structured development process. Figure 5–3 shows an example of a typical generic process. The generic development process for a particular company will vary somewhat depending on the type of product being developed, markets into which the product is sold, product uniqueness from a technical and marketing perspective, product complexity, organizational structure, and culture in place.

The generic structure is used to define a specific project overview for each project. Project overviews clearly delineate the major steps of product development and the phase-review points at the end of each phase. At this time steps are specifically estimated and schedule dates are added to the overview.

The entire company should see and understand this high-level, one-page overview. It becomes the vision for the project. If the project cannot be laid out simply on one page, then it cannot be clearly understood by those doing it or managing it. From executive management to first-year designer, everyone should know the steps in the process and how they all fit together.

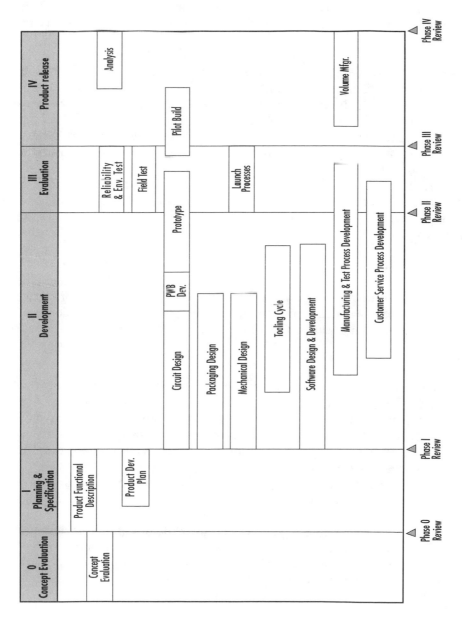

FIGURE 5–3   Product development structure.

Steps

Steps are the most critical level within a structured process. They are the basis of scheduling and provide the link between phases and detailed tasks and activities. It is critical that they be properly defined. If steps are not properly defined, then a company will be unable to achieve a significant improvement in time-to-market. The definition of the process itself could constrain product development activity by requiring excessive non-value-added activity, stifling concurrent engineering and teamwork, or sequencing activity inefficiently.

One company, for example, asked an experienced engineer to define the steps in its product development process. When he completed the definition, the company's CEO directed that everyone in the company follow the steps as defined. Although his intent was to reduce time-to-market, because the steps were not properly defined, time-to-market actually increased.

The steps in a structured development process should be clearly defined and consistently applied. Take the functional specification step, for example. Everyone should know what the functional specification includes, how comprehensive it is, how long it takes to develop, and when it is scheduled in the design process. It becomes common terminology, and the emphasis can be on execution. Steps define the deliverables expected during or at the end of the step as well as the review points, such as design reviews, that are part of that step.

Steps should be consistently applied to all product development projects. Product specifications, for example, should be done at the specified time in the schedule, with the same scope and to the same level of detail from project to project. Senior management can then rely on the specification being done and understand what it includes.

Tasks and Activities

Each step consists of a number of tasks that define more specifically how that step is done. The flow of tasks not only defines what needs to be done but outlines the sequence as well. Figure 5–4 shows a sample flow of tasks for a typical software design step. This begins with a task to review software requirements developed in a previous step and goes through the tasks required to complete and review the software design.

The task level within structured software development also defines how the development is to be done. The software design example implements a structured software development approach by defining that high-level design be done and reviewed before module design. Module design and review will then be performed. The example also shows that the proper planning for testing be done simultaneously rather than when coding is complete. As a result, the company can implement a more disciplined approach to product development, where the design is completed and reviewed before coding.

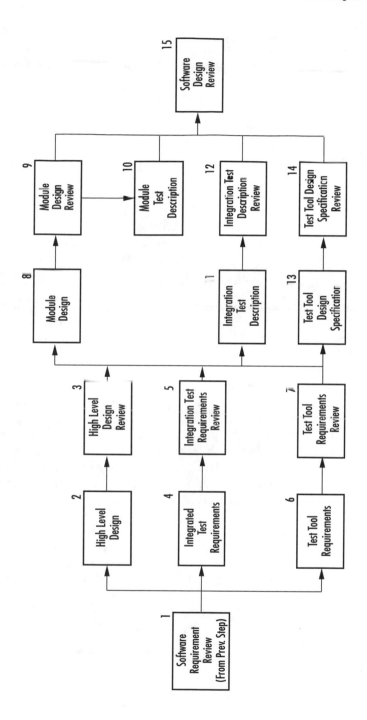

FIGURE 5-4 Sample tasks for software design step.

Detailed Development Guidelines

The focus on "how to" is important in order to leverage the product development learning experience. For example, a manufacturer of discrete semiconductors had detailed guidelines of what was to be done, but only the most experienced development managers knew how to do it. This company's growth was limited by the amount of senior management time available to help people learn the process. Consequently, senior managers spent all their time in development instead of running the business.

Guidelines for the development process provide many benefits to an organization, including the following:

- Capturing learning across multiple projects
- Increasing proactive up-front thinking as opposed to fire fighting
- Establishing a starting point for process measurement and improvement
- Enabling scheduling based on what the process is capable of producing, instead of speculation about process capabilities

The intent of process guidelines is to capture the present knowledge that exists in people's heads or in filing cabinets. If each project uses guidelines for implementation, people quickly begin to find better ways of conducting product development. These improvements can then be reflected in continuous updates of the guidelines so that every project can incorporate these new methods. Guidelines help capture this learning on an ongoing basis.

At the start of a development effort, the Core Team should use the latest version of the guidelines as an aid in planning the project. Each team member should review his or her respective guidelines and identify any potential problems or high-risk areas. These can then be reflected in the team's development plan.

A company must carefully consider the type of guidelines and level of detail required before guideline creation. Development guidelines can range from simple one-page flowcharts and checklists to detailed descriptions of critical activities. The style and depth will depend on the company's culture, complexity of products, and markets.

The test for all guidelines is a simple one: they must be readily adopted and easily used by development teams. If every project is not using the guidelines, then the guidelines must be changed because people will eventually circumvent them. When all projects use the guidelines, problems and bottlenecks with the current methodology can be quickly identified. Addressing these problems one by one will assist an organization to become world class in new product development.

Scheduling with Structured Development

Few people would challenge the importance of creating a schedule for product development work and managing activity to such a schedule, but most people don't like schedules or understand how to successfully create one that works. A good schedule is critical to reaching the market window on time. It becomes the focus of control and a means of communicating progress to the entire project team.

Scheduling product development is difficult for several reasons. First, many details about the development are undetermined. Despite this, many companies push development teams to commit to an end date before they have even completed the design specification. Once the team commits, even if it has laid out all of its assumptions, management tends to lock in on a crude estimated date and can't understand why later, when the project scope is better defined, the estimated date no longer holds. We frequently hear management telling teams that "you haven't even started and already you're eight weeks late."

Scheduling is also difficult because resources are not always available when the team really needs them. Typically, time is lost waiting for the right people or tools to become available.

Finally, most people are too optimistic when asked: Can you do this by such and such a date? It's not that people are inherently dishonest, it's just that many of us don't schedule with correct capacities in mind. If, for instance, a normal work week is 50 hours for a development professional, then to do a schedule based on a 50-hour-per-week availability is unrealistic because it doesn't take into account vacation, sick time, training, administrative tasks, and assisting on other projects. These activities must be accounted for, leaving the remaining time as that which is available for new work.

Three-Level Scheduling

Product development has become so complex that the standard approach of one person creating, managing, and controlling a development project plan no longer works. Techniques such as critical path method (CPM) and project evaluation review technique (PERT) are inadequate for product development. Development is essentially an information flow; a physical entity is often not realized until the prototype-build stage. Because techniques such as PERT and CPM were created primarily for physical flows, they are insufficient for managing product development successfully.

PRTM developed the three-level scheduling technique specifically for product development. It uses structured development as the basis for developing and managing schedules. Product development calls for dissemination of information at three levels. Three-level scheduling enables varying levels of project-management detail for different audiences. Managing an inappropriate level of detail frequently results in either poor decision making or micromanagement of the design team. Recognizing this problem, three-level scheduling uses a different amount of detail for different audiences: an overview chart for senior management, a step schedule with task detail for the Core Team, and a task schedule with activity detail for individual Core Team members and the full project team working on these tasks.

Cycle-Time Guidelines

Cycle-time guidelines form the basis for project scheduling in world-class product development companies. Cycle-time guidelines characterize a company's product development process from a time perspective. They are established at the step level and vary based on the characteristics of the product being developed. For instance, mechanical design cycle times for low-, medium-, and high-complexity products can be captured over time and used as the basis for estimation on new projects.

Project schedules can then be estimated by breaking the project down to the step level and categorizing the product and project in terms of such characteristics as complexity, technical risk, and scope. Step cycle times can then be estimated using these characteristics from a data base of cycle times. The overall project schedule is then completed using these step cycle times as building blocks.

Cycle-time guidelines provide an accurate method for developing reliable project schedules. Using them to develop step estimates, then using those estimates to generate accurate and predictable schedules, often boosts management's confidence in the team. Discussions between individual Core Teams and management focus on technical content and complexity instead of arguments over how much schedules are padded.

Cycle-time guidelines allow management to focus on the complexity of the product being developed. Discussions between management and Core Teams are no longer based on how much the schedule has been padded or how much management will arbitrarily cut out. Rather, everyone focuses on the characteristics of what has to be done.

Finally, cycle-time guidelines are a way to see whether the process is being continually improved. World-class companies revise their cycle-time guidelines at least once a year because actual development times are continually being reduced.

Why Some Companies Haven't Been Successful in Structuring Their Product Development Process

Many companies have tried in some way to define the activities of their product development process in order to get some control over it. Yet many have not achieved the potential benefits because of problems like the following:

- They have defined all the product development activities, but have not defined any structure for them.
- The process may not be structured appropriately to enable decision making at one level, planning and scheduling at the next, and task management at the lowest level.
- The levels of the process may not be integrated.

- The process may not have been effectively implemented.
- The process structure may not include standard cycle times for project scheduling.
- The process may be overly defined and bureaucratic, typically requiring numerous documents to justify completion.

CHAPTER 6

Design Techniques and Automated Development Tools

Michael T. Anthony

Historically, improvements to the product development process have focused on the application of various design techniques and automated development tools. Often touted as "silver bullets," these tools and techniques promised dramatic improvements in time-to-market, product quality, and engineering productivity. Unfortunately, many companies investing in a specific tool or technique found that improvements were minimal. Often the disappointing results were attributed to flaws in the tool or technique, when in reality fault was due to improper implementation.

PACE looks at product development as a process with many aspects that should be improved, not as something that can be fixed by the application of a single tool or technique. Techniques such as quality function deployment (QFD) and the various techniques encompassed by design for excellence (DFE) can dramatically improve product development, but only when correctly applied within a structured process. Automated design tools can be used to support Core Team effectiveness through improvements in design in specific functional areas and through integration of the technical aspects of product development.

After a company has implemented the basic elements of PACE (Core Teams, Phase Review Process, and a structured development process), the appropriate application of specific tools and techniques can lead to a continued reduction in time-to-market and lower life-cycle costs. Applying these tools and techniques before the basic elements of PACE are functioning will only lead to disappointment.

Design Techniques

Several major design techniques have been developed with the objective of improving the effectiveness and productivity of design professionals. The major techniques include QFD, the array of techniques encompassed by DFE (design for assembly, manufacturability, testability, serviceability, international, and green) and user-oriented design. Each technique, when properly applied within the context of PACE, can lead to additional improvements in the product development process.

Simplified Quality Function Deployment

QFD is a technique originally developed during the 1970s by the Kobe Shipyard in Japan. It is a disciplined approach to planning, communicating, and documenting customer requirements and translating them into design activities. Many excellent books and articles on QFD explain the concept.[1,2]

Traditional QFD focused on detailed elements of a relatively simple product. Capturing customer requirements and design alternatives was straightforward and did not take much time. However, when attempting to apply the technique to complex system products, PRTM found classical QFD to be quite cumbersome and time-consuming. We spent almost two years modifying the basic QFD approach so that it would work effectively with more complex products.

When there are many elements to consider, for example in a systems product containing many hardware and software subsystems, different customer requirements, a high degree of complexity, and short life cycles, applying QFD could even lengthen time-to-market. The value of QFD quickly diminishes after identifying high-level requirements and prioritizing them. If the problem is complex, it is easy to get lost in the process of a QFD analysis. For example, design teams at one company found that their lists of customer requirements and technical approaches often resulted in matrices that had hundreds of columns and rows, leading to thousands of cells to evaluate. Clearly a new and different approach was required. PRTM developed simplified quality function deployment, or S-QFD, in 1989 and has since refined and applied the technique on many complex technology-based products.[3]

Design for Excellence (DFE)

The three most important new product factors from the customer's standpoint are quality, cost, and delivery. New product quality means a consistently good product with high reliability. Customers would like to know when they purchase the product that they don't have to worry about whether it works properly. High quality is expected. The quality of a new product depends heavily on the product's design.

Product cost depends quite heavily on the materials and manufacturability of the design. All too often, we see products canceled before production because their cost is so high that the price would be unbearable. Considering cost as a design objective is critical to acceptance by the customer.

Finally, customers want their new products on time, every time. Today few companies can get by on the old technique of announcing that their new product will be available next quarter, only to slip the introduction another six months. Ongoing delivery depends heavily on the parts and assembly processes specified by the product's design.

Managing these factors is the goal of DFE. DFE means incorporating considerations other than pure product performance into the product design. This is ultimately done to lower the life-cycle cost of the product and therefore increase profitability. Some of the following design considerations are typical:

- *Assembly* — making the product easier to assemble, thereby reducing cycle time during production
- *Manufacturability* — maximizing ease of manufacture by minimizing complexity through part-count reduction and related techniques
- *Testability* — designing the product so that it can be effectively and efficiently tested
- *Serviceability* — minimizing the number of service calls and downtime per call
- *International* — designing for international roll-out
- *Green* — designing environmentally conscious products

Design for assembly

Design for assembly (DFA) focuses on simplifying the assembly process, which ultimately reduces manufacturing time and improves product quality. This means designing the product so that its assembly is as foolproof as possible, because every bit of handling during the assembly process has the potential to introduce errors and variation.

The entire fabrication, subassembly, and assembly process must be as clear as possible. Components should be designed so that they can only be assembled in one way. Cutouts, notches, asymmetrical holes, and stops are some of the ways to foolproof the assembly process by design.

Design for manufacturability

Design for manufacturability (DFM) seeks to maximize ease of manufacture by simplifying the design through part-count reduction. Reducing the number of parts is important. Each part in a product means an opportunity to introduce defects and assembly errors. As part counts are reduced, the probability of a high-quality product increases exponentially. Fewer parts also means higher reliability, lower life-cycle costs, less design engineering labor (including less redesign), and less purchasing, quality assurance labor, and fewer stores, as well as less floor space.

An American systems company received a rude awakening about the need for DFM. A Japanese competitor came into the market with the same features and performance as the American company's current, top-of-the-line product but with a reduced part count (see Figure 6–1). The American company had to quickly redesign its product to be cost competitive with the Japanese product. Fortunately, it was able to complete a DFM analysis and greatly improve its product before losing too much market share.

Cost reduction is another major reason to institute DFM. The cost of the part is obviously zero if it's eliminated, but so are the associated costs of purchasing, stocking, and servicing that part. To determine the theoretical minimum number of parts required in a new design, ask the following questions: Does the part move relative to all other moving parts? Does it absolutely have to be made of a different material from the other parts? Does the part have to be different to allow for product disassembly?

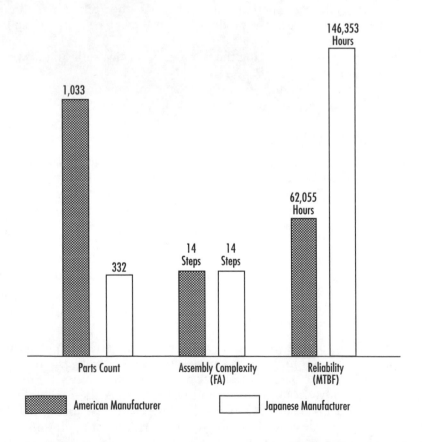

FIGURE 6–1 Measuring performance — comparison of two digital data communication products.

Design for testability

The goal of design for testability (DFT) is to design a product so that the necessary tests can be efficiently generated and completed in the shortest amount of time. The testability of a design is indicated by the percentage of functionality covered by test nodes, but 100% coverage is usually an impossible goal. The effectiveness of trying to write additional test vectors is limited by the size and complexity of the product.

Test development has always been an expensive headache for product development teams. As designs increase in complexity, it can be expected that developing test programs will require more and more of the development budget and schedule. For some companies, it can take from six months to a year to develop a test program that will test the product sufficiently. The alternative — inadequate test coverage — can lead to dissatisfied customers and a product or company with a tarnished industry image. Because of this, DFT is becoming increasingly important.

Also included in this is the concept of loosely coupled designs, wherein modules can be effectively tested in isolation and only a few tests need to be done to check the integration of the modules. In tightly coupled designs, many interactions have to be tested and a hierarchical approach cannot be taken. Also, tightly coupled designs tend to have many more combinations and paths to test, making comprehensive testing lengthy or impossible. An example is a recent TV software development in which the use of a loosely coupled design reduced the test cycle time from two or three days down to two or three hours.

Design for serviceability

Design for serviceability (DFS) means considering during the design cycle how the product will be serviced in the field. For low-cost products, DFS can be as simple as determining the cost of repair versus the cost of total replacement. For larger and more expensive products, however, serviceability is an important issue. Customers obviously don't want products that break down, and if something does go wrong they want their systems up and running as fast as possible.

Some companies are incorporating diagnostic capabilities into their designs. Digital Equipment Corporation, for example, spent hundreds of millions of dollars in artificial intelligence systems for diagnostics. Theoretically, these systems are so advanced that they can predict when a specific part of a customer's system is going to break down, order a replacement part, and get it in the customer's hands before the failure actually occurs.

Design for international

Design for international (DFI) seeks to manage the design process in such a way that the product can be quickly adapted into each particular country or market in which it is sold with a minimal amount of work. Minimizing the cost of international customization is what DFI is all about.

One of the best examples of DFI is the Xerox 5100 copier. Introduced in 1990, the 5100 was the first jointly developed product, a collaboration between Fuji Xerox of Japan and Xerox Corporation engineers. The requirements of a successful copier product in Japan differ greatly from those in the United States. For example, Japanese paper is a lighter weight and has a smoother finish, Kanji characters are much more complex and intricate, and the use of blue pencil lead is common. In the past, these factors meant that unique products had to be developed for each market. This led, of course, to each of these products being reengineered to fit the needs of other markets.

By employing DFI considerations, Xerox designed the 5100 series concurrently from concept to delivery. Input for the design was collected from customer groups in the United States, Europe, and Japan. The 5100 was introduced to the Japanese market in November 1990 and in the United States in February 1991. It was the fastest global roll-out for any new product yet at Xerox. This DFI approach saved Xerox more than $10 million in development costs.

Design for green

Design for green (DFG) considers the design of the product (and the manufacturing process) from an environmental standpoint. Many companies are becoming increasingly aware of the impact of their products and associated manufacturing processes on the environment. DFG seeks to reduce pollutants from the manufacturing process by eliminating hazardous by-products or shifting to benign by-products. DFG also strives to minimize the environmental impact of the product after its useful life through recycling or allowing the product to safely decompose.

Some companies have made considerable DFG progress. Carrier Corporation spent $500,000 in 1988 to remove toxic lubricants from its manufacturing process, resulting in an annual production savings of $1.2 million by avoiding hazardous waste disposal costs. AT&T removed an ozone-depleting compound from its circuit board manufacturing process and saved $3 million annually. Polaroid recently eliminated mercury from its batteries, making its production environment safer and protecting the environment after the consumer throws away the battery.

As demonstrated by these examples, not only is DFG environmentally conscious, but often it can also lower manufacturing costs by eliminating the hidden costs associated with health problems and hazardous waste handling and disposal. Health claims are tremendously high for miners with black lung disease and for people who have had long-term exposure to asbestos. The same problems may confront the electronics industry because of the many hazardous chemicals used; for example, chemical exposure in the manufacture of printed circuit boards. DFG also minimizes the need for hazardous waste disposal, the costs of which continue to rise as waste sites fill and the public becomes alarmed, leading to increased government regulation.

User-Oriented Design

One of the challenges in the design of today's electronic products is allowing the user to take full advantage of the power and features possible with the advances in microprocessors and software. How many times have we encountered a VCR with the clock flashing "12:00" incessantly? How many of us have sat down with an IBM PC (before Windows 3.0) and tried to remember the arcane commands needed to manipulate files? These are just two of a myriad of occasions when product design has not been user oriented.

User-oriented design focuses on how the user interacts with the product (that is, the user interface). This is especially critical as products grow in terms of complexity and capability. User-oriented design includes all of the ways in which people can interact with a product:

- *Operation* — the way the product is used every day
- *Installation* — the time from receiving the product until it is fully operational
- *Documentation* — clear and simple description of technical functions
- *User training* — quick and painless instruction on how to use the product
- *Customer repair* — the ability of the user to easily diagnose and repair the product

User-oriented design is becoming increasingly important as products grow in complexity. Software companies in particular find that user-oriented design pays off in terms of quicker market acceptance, leading to more customers.

Several factors driving user-oriented design include compatibility with other products (including those of competitors), increasingly comprehensive industry standards (formal and de facto), and the transition from technically knowledgeable customers to those who want to "plug and play." In other words, today's customers don't care about the technical details of the product; they simply want it to work.

One of the best examples of user-oriented design is the Apple Macintosh computer, which has always been differentiated by its user friendliness. That its product margins are among the highest in the industry is no coincidence. Introduced in the mid-1980s, the Mac is still the easiest computer to use, without any fundamental design changes. Installation consists of plugging the unit in and switching it on, and instantly the user is in the Mac's "desktop." Arcane operating system commands are replaced by intuitively understandable icons. A mouse allows the user to move naturally around the screen instead of being confined by directional keys. All application programs have the same look and feel (pull-down menus, scroll bars, common key words), so that if the user has learned one program, learning others is simple. In the past few years, all major computer and software manufacturers have attempted to duplicate the Mac's ease-of-use, which has set the de facto industry standard for graphical user interface.

Design Technique Timing

Even though DFE techniques are powerful, their effectiveness relies on correct placement within the structured development process, as shown in Figure 6–2.

- S-QFD takes customer input (Phase 0) and translates it into technical specifications (Phase I), then converts these into a product design (Phase II). The importance of S-QFD diminishes greatly after detailed design has begun.
- With user interface often integral to the product concept, user-oriented design is undertaken early in development.
- International design considerations often affect the fundamentals of a product's design; therefore, DFI must begin before product specifications are finalized.
- Environmental considerations lead to DFG decisions affecting the basic materials and configuration of the product determined during Phase I.
- DFA, DFM, and DFS can start only when rough specifications are in place, thus allowing trade-offs to be made between specific aspects of the product's design.
- DFT is applied later in development, when the design is sufficiently complete to determine and thus optimize specific testing requirements.

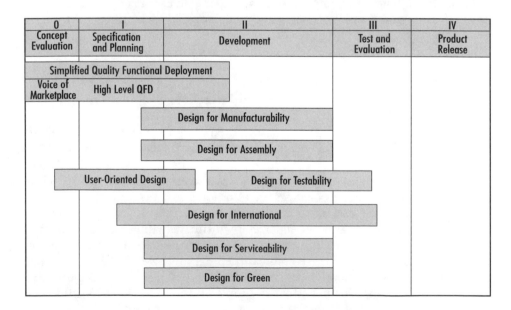

0	I	II	III	IV
Concept Evaluation	Specification and Planning	Development	Test and Evaluation	Product Release

FIGURE 6–2   Design technique positioning within the structured development process.

Ultimately, these techniques should be seamlessly integrated into a company's PACE process guidelines.

Automated Tools for Product Development

Once properly structured, the product development process can benefit greatly from the implementation of automated product development tools. These tools can accelerate and in some cases completely eliminate development tasks. A wide range of development tools can accelerate product development activities. For the sake of convenience in illustrating how they apply, we will use four categories: design tools, simulation tools, development tools, and project management and execution tools.

Design Tools

Automated design tools can play an important role in accelerating the early tasks of the product design process. They generally focus on the engineering or behavioral aspects of how the product or subsystem will function, based on key inputs and expected outputs. By allowing engineers to quickly conduct "what-ifs" or a scenario analysis of desired functionality, they reduce the time required to determine the optimal design alternative. This capability also allows an engineer to test the limits of various design approaches on an automated design workstation before delving into the next layer of design. Examining several types of design tools illustrates these benefits.

Electrical design tools

Electrical design tools translate a design specification into an output package for circuit board development. Design tools can be applied to most of the tasks in the hardware design process. They are valuable for completing design specifications, controlling documentation, performing behavioral-level modeling, analyzing part selection, creating schematics, simulating the design, developing net lists, and generating parts lists.

Automating these tools can save a significant amount of time. Additionally, the automated process can avoid many typical errors that affect later steps in the process.

Computer-aided software engineering

Computer-aided software engineering (CASE) tools facilitate the application of engineering work methods to the process of developing software. Simply put, CASE tools are automated tools for the planning, analysis, and design of software. They eliminate many of the lower-level, mundane tasks (such as data base definition or screen generation), allowing people to focus on software design before coding.

CASE hides much of this lower-level detail from the user within its own set of generated routines. This allows designers to concentrate on what they want to do instead of the details of how to do it. Thus, CASE allows software professionals to spend more time ensuring that requirements are clearly established and that the design of the system is approached properly instead of jumping into the coding task.

Mechanical design tools

Mechanical design tools are becoming increasingly important in industries such as consumer electronics, wherein the look of a product tends to change every six to twelve months. These tools can truly speed up the mechanical design process. Every type of design can be modularized and stored in a mechanical design component library. When developing a new product, the mechanical or industrial design engineer can then pull the desired modules out of the data base and modify them for a new product, rather than start from scratch.

The development of design tools for mechanical and industrial design has lagged behind that of electrical design tools by eight to ten years. Recently, however, as a result of the increasing power of workstations and personal computers, mechanical design tools have made important advances. They are no longer just two-dimensional electronic drafting boards.

Some tools even have the capability to create the mold patterns for the product. These then can be electronically transferred to the tooling vendor's system for review and modification during the tooling development cycle.

Simulation Tools

Designers simulate the mechanical or electrical portion of a design to analyze and evaluate the operational characteristics of the design to see if it will function as desired. Design tools conduct simulation by executing a software model that represents the specific product subsystem to be built.

Simulation shortens the design cycle by quickly verifying that a particular design approach is feasible. Simulating the design also tends to reduce the need for extensive prototyping, lowers test programming time, and reduces debugging time at hardware/software integration testing.

The design of an electronic product can be simulated at many levels: component, circuit, board, or system. Today most companies can simulate their electrical designs to the printed circuit board level, although a few very large companies have developed the ability to simulate the functionality of highly complex systems. Most companies, however, cannot afford the hardware and complex software programs to simulate at the systems level.

One data communications manufacturer first employed simulation tools early in 1991. It found that an experienced user was able to eliminate one prototype cycle, thus saving twelve weeks of design time. In addition, simulation also allowed users to routinely shave eight to ten weeks from design verification time.

Development Tools

Automated development tools are used to translate a high-level design into an output file for fabrication. These tools quickly complete some of the mundane and time-intensive tasks of developing a new product and therefore reduce development time. This can be illustrated by looking at two types of development tools in use today.

Integrated-circuit or printed-circuit-board development tools

Integrated-circuit or printed-circuit-board development tools are typically used by a separate CAD department downstream from the electrical-design engineers. The input for these tools is the output package from design engineering tools and includes schematics, a net list, and logic block diagrams. Development tools are used to turn this information into a completed integrated circuit (IC) or printed-circuit-board development file for fabrication.

These development tools automate the placement of components on the circuit board or substrate, then route the interconnections between the components themselves and the input/output connections on the board or chip. These tools are also used to conduct analysis of power consumption and thermal tolerance of the components and associated circuitry to avoid problems with the design. Automating this step can cut weeks from a design cycle time and reduce errors. Many also incorporate design rule checkers to prevent users from inadvertently designing a product that won't function, and some also include manufacturability considerations for ease of manufacture.

Rapid prototyping

Rapid prototyping is one of the fastest growing design-tool areas. Systems have recently been developed that can create a physical prototype within hours or a couple of days (based on a part's size and complexity). Ordinarily this process could take many weeks or even months.

Rapid-prototyping tools also give designers a quick method of seeing and handling a part that closely approximates the final product. These rapid prototypes can be put to many advantageous uses, such as:

- Debugging early designs
- Eliminating more expensive early prototypes
- Checking form and fit of mating parts
- Testing air and liquid flow, thermal, stiffness, and mechanical properties
- Modeling hard-to-visualize sections of the design
- Spotlighting dimensional errors
- Demonstrating manufacturability problems
- Testing customer reaction to new industrial designs

Project Management and Execution Tools

Automated tools can also assist in improving project management and execution. Properly used, they can accelerate product development even more. Typical of such tools are those used for project scheduling, new product financial analysis, video conferencing, and groupware.

Project scheduling tools

Project scheduling tools automate project planning and tracking. More than one hundred project scheduling software packages are available on the market today. They can relieve the Core Team from the manual process of keeping track of tasks and activities; the generation of Gantt-type charts can be especially helpful. Many of these tools can perform project scheduling in a layered fashion, wherein individual schedules can be created for elements of the design and then rolled up into an overall schedule. Some can provide an overall vision chart of the entire project.

Project-scheduling tools are not a blueprint for project management. We find this to be a common mistake. Typically this happens when a project team is not given any guidance on how to manage projects. It uses project-management software that automates many techniques and manages its project without deciding which techniques are most appropriate.

We find that the best tools for project scheduling are those that are easy to use from three perspectives. First, the tool should allow quick and easy development of a project schedule. Second, it must be even easier to update or revise the schedule. Finally, the tool must generate clean, easy-to-read reports.

Financial analysis tools

Financial analysis tools automate financial projections. In the early phases of product development, projecting the expected sales and financial analysis is a critical activity of the Core Team. With the popularity of PC-based spreadsheet tools, this task is now much easier. A truly effective tool, however, needs to go one step further and create standard templates for new product planning and financial analysis.

We have seen many project teams design their own formats for this financial analysis. They spend more time putting together the worksheet than they do validating their assumptions. As a result, the output looks nice, but the input was not thought through. Additionally, when the worksheets are presented to the Product Approval Committee, or PAC, the formats and analysis vary from project to project, making the PAC's job more difficult. The solution is to standardize this tool using a template.

Video conferencing

Video conferencing is a project management tool that is being increasingly accepted by product development teams that are geographically dispersed. One telecommunications company, for example, has marketing on the East Coast, R&D in California, a circuit-board manufacturing plant in Taiwan, and systems assembly in Mexico. Running a weekly face-to-face Core Team meeting would be impossible or prohibitively expensive. With the use of video conferencing, the company is able to conduct meetings effectively in what approximates a real situation.

Video conferencing tools allow people to see each other even though they may be located in another state or country. This capability is a great improvement over teleconferencing, which is limited to audio. With video conferencing the Core Team can work on-line to solve problems, manage the schedule, conduct design or documentation reviews, and improve communications among functions.

Groupware

Groupware tools are still in their infancy, but look for the number of applications and vendors to grow rapidly in the 1990s. Groupware tools such as Lotus Notes allow members of a work group, such as a Core Team, to work on or edit the same document in parallel. For example, if a team is working on a functional specification or product development plan, all team members can generate sections of it and make edits concurrently. Some groupware tools have voice-note annotation so that while a person is making revisions, he or she can listen to inserted audio comments, questions, or advice from team members who are concurrently involved in creating it.

Common Problems in Implementing Automated Development Tools

To take full advantage of what design tools have to offer, it is important to avoid some common traps into which many companies fall. Most of these problems can be avoided through careful planning and requirements definition before the tools are implemented.

The most common mistake, in our experience, has been to attempt to implement design tools without first structuring the product development process. The result is the ability to execute a very inefficient process faster, thus compounding inefficiencies.

Many managers have unrealistic expectations of what tools can accomplish. A learning curve is associated with any design tool, and some tools take much longer to learn than others. One systems company vice president didn't understand this. His design engineers became extremely frustrated at his demands to get the new design done in half the time because he had spent tens of thousands of dollars investing in electrical design tools. The lead engineer told us "he thinks that there are three buttons on the workstation. Press button one and the design is complete, press button two and we have six-sigma quality, then press button three and we beat the schedule." If only it were that easy.

Not understanding the supporting infrastructure required to use design tools effectively is another major problem. Just buying a design tool and plugging it in won't give a company any advantage. The users have to be trained in the tool and all of its capabilities; maintenance and control procedures have to be established; libraries must be either purchased and installed or specifically created; and resources have to be trained or hired to manage the design tool implementation. Failure to consider these factors adequately will result in tools that are not used or used with no benefit derived from purchasing them.

Maintaining the integrity of a tool's data base is critical to its ability to add value to the design process. Many companies make the mistake of treating this lightly. Typically, what happens then is that a multitude of components get added to the data base. Many are redundant, some are outright wrong, and few are correctly documented. This of course creates a distrust of the data base; in reaction, various design groups create their own data bases and libraries. It doesn't take long for the entire process to get out of hand.

Another typical problem is for companies to procure new design tools to address a specific problem, such as circuit board layout or mechanical design. Until recently, many tools optimized one element of the design process and inadequately addressed others. Electrical design tool vendors, for example, have had either great behavioral-level modeling and simulation capabilities or good circuit-board placement and routing development abilities, but not both. This led to designers purchasing tools from one vendor and the CAD group selecting a different vendor. The problem then becomes how to integrate these tools to avoid manual manipulation of data.

Not selecting a common hardware platform has also been a major problem. Before UNIX became so prevalent in the industry, it was not uncommon to walk into a mid-sized corporation and find multiple hardware platforms in the design area. The problem here is that design tool applications typically could not be swapped back and forth to run on Sun, Apollo, IBM, DEC, and Hewlett Packard hardware.

Why Some Companies Haven't Been Successful in Applying Design Techniques and Automated Tools

Design techniques and automated tools frequently fall short of achieving their intended benefits. Some of the reasons for this are:

- Techniques and tools are applied at the wrong point in the development process.
- Successful application is dependent on other tasks in the development process, and these other tasks are deficient.
- The techniques and tools are promoted by individual functional departments, thereby increasing functional barriers.

- Some people within the company have unrealistic expectations that the technique or tool can solve all problems.
- The wrong technique or tool is applied.
- The technique or tool is not properly implemented.

References

1. Yoji Akao, *Quality Function Deployment-QFD* (Cambridge, Mass: Productivity Press, 1990).
2. William E. Eureka and Nancy E. Ryan, *The Customer-Driven Company: Managerial Perspectives on QFD* (Dearborn, Michigan: ASI Press, a division of American Supplier Institute, Inc., 1988).
3. For more information on S-QFD, see Michael T. Anthony, "Simplified QFD for High-Technology Product Development," *Visions, PDMA* (March 1995).

CHAPTER 7

The Process of Product Strategy

Mark J. Deck
Michael E. McGrath

Every company would like to have a brilliant product strategy that enables it to enter an emerging market before anyone else or one that provides it with a continuous stream of competitively superior products. An effective product strategy can inspire the development of successful products, while an ineffective product strategy can make even the best development efforts a waste of time. Brilliant or ineffective, product strategy is the starting point for product development, and it affects product development in many important ways.

Product strategy provides a strategic-level perspective of product opportunities. Without this perspective, a company is forced to make decisions on new products and new generations of existing products without seeing the entire spectrum of opportunities. Mediocre products may be developed while better opportunities are overlooked. But with an effective product strategy, a company can be confident that it has considered all major opportunities before selecting its new product investments.

Product strategy provides the link between a company's overall business strategy and product development decisions. In PACE, it is implemented through decisions made in the Phase Review Process by determining which opportunities enter Phase 0 and by influencing which projects receive resource priority.

It is frequently in the Phase Review Process that the need for a better product strategy is identified. This happens when a company's senior executives, the Product Approval Committee (PAC), are faced with a phase review decision on a new product and find that they do not have a clear product strategy on

101

which to base their decision. They struggle to establish priorities while feeling uncertain about having identified the best opportunities.

Product strategy provides a road map to where product development is going. Without it there is no context for product developers, who end up defining products without an understanding of where each fits into the company's future plans. Each new product proposal becomes a knee-jerk response to changes in the market. Instead of being competitively positioned, products typically have too many or even the wrong features. Product definition takes place one product at a time, rather than as part of a coordinated strategy. The result is a patchwork of individual products rather than an integrated product line.

A clear product strategy encourages proactive rather than reactive product development by systematically mapping out future product development activities in advance, anticipating market and technical changes. It also identifies the needs and priorities for development of technology, manufacturing, and service so that a company can effectively extend and leverage its core capabilities.

Product strategy is a management process. Better product strategy results from a better product strategy process. Conceptually, product strategy is based on four levels, as shown in Figure 7–1. Each level has distinctly different characteristics, and the development of product strategy tends to flow from top to bottom, from general to specific.

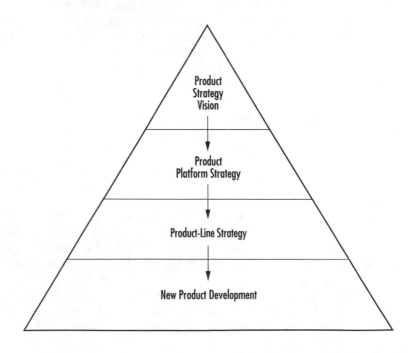

FIGURE 7–1   Product strategy process structure.

A product strategy vision is at the top of this structure. It guides the nature, timing, and competitive positioning of product platform strategy at the next level. Product line strategy is derived from the product platform strategy and the development of individual products is the execution of the product line strategy.

Product Strategy Vision

Product strategy begins with a clear strategic vision that provides context and direction. It guides those developing the individual elements of a product strategy by describing to them where the company is going, how it expects to get there, and why it can be successful.

Companies with an exceptional vision of their product strategy can achieve unusual success. They clearly know where they are going and how they will get there. They are confident that they will be successful, and they move decisively. There is no debate or argument about contradictory directions. There is no confusion about what to do or how to do it. They determine their product strategies to achieve their visions and then execute these strategies.

Product strategic vision serves several essential purposes:

1. *It focuses the efforts of those responsible for identifying new product opportunities.* The strategic vision tells them the direction toward which they should look for new opportunities. With a strategic vision, they begin to consider the right opportunities from the start. Without a vision, they come up with diverse ideas for new products that may be inconsistent with the company's strengths or direction. While potentially creative, a myriad of inappropriate opportunities distracts a company and dilutes scarce resources.

For example, one consumer electronics company pursued an opportunity in broadcasting largely on the basis of expected profitability. After investing a significant amount of time and money to initiate development, the company finally decided that the opportunity did not fit its strategic vision. In the meantime, it had neglected other opportunities that would have better used its skills. Competitors focused on directly related opportunities and benefited from the company's distraction.

2. *It establishes a framework for product platform strategy.* Product strategy vision guides the nature, timing, and competitive positioning of product platforms. Without a strategic vision, product platform strategy is unguided. One company's dilemma illustrates this problem.

A computer company sent a team to an off-site location to conceive the next generation of products. With virtually no direction from or communication with top management, the team spent two months being creative, pushing the limits of technology. They came back with a product platform concept that was a complete departure from the company's direction toward smaller, more competitive systems. The proposal was rejected, and the team was asked to start from scratch, guided by a clearer divisional product strategy vision.

3. *It guides product development activities.* Those working directly on new products are more successful if they know where the company is going and how it expects to get there. This helps them to make design-level decisions consistent with the strategic vision. A clear strategic vision helps align product development activities in a common direction. In particular, the strategic vision establishes the key vectors of differentiation that will guide competitive positioning and performance goals.

If those developing products do not understand the company's vision, they make guesses about it or make it up themselves. This leads to organizationally inverted responsibilities. The product developers often determine the company product strategy vision by default because the CEO and senior executives are too busy fighting fires and making detailed product design decisions.

An effective product strategy vision also motivates people to make innovative breakthroughs. If Core Teams have a clear, market-driven performance goal and are confident about the future viability of that direction, they will put in the extra effort to ensure that the company gets there with its new products. Nothing helps a development team to jell more quickly than a crisp, well-thought-out strategic vision. However, if a development team lacks confidence in a company's vision, it is difficult to get it to put in the extra effort.

4. *It provides direction for technology development and other critical business functions.* A clear product strategy vision helps to set the general agenda for technology development. This can include R&D, information technology, manufacturing technology, and even channel development. It suggests the technical competencies that will enable a company to succeed. By going through a formal process to develop a clear product strategy vision, one company completely changed the direction of its research, based on its newly clarified vision. It canceled a significant research program that did not support its new vision, initiated research in two new areas where it needed additional technical competencies to achieve this vision, and launched a technical monitoring program to watch some potential emerging technologies that could have an impact on its vision.

5. *It sets expectations for customers, employees, and investors.* A clear strategic vision is the best way to communicate to these groups where the company is going. If they believe in the vision, they will enthusiastically support the company. If they do not, they may abandon it. However, without a vision, their support may be unpredictable. Communicating the strategic vision creates a dilemma. If a company tells everyone its strategic vision, competitors will also learn about it. This points out one of the differences between strategic vision and product strategy. The vision does not describe specific details. While it can be of some help to competitors, it is not specific competitive intelligence.

A complete product strategy vision statement must answer three questions: Where is the company going? How will it get there? Why will it be successful?

Strategic visions are developed at the business-unit or division level, not the corporate level. Trying to develop a strategic vision at the corporate level of a large diversified company is usually ineffective. Its business units are usually too different to pursue the same vision. Responsibility for a product strategy vision rests clearly with the CEO or head of the business unit. This does not mean that he or she develops that vision without input from others. On the contrary, it's usually a mistake to develop a vision in a vacuum.

Product Platform Strategy

Product platform strategy is the next level of the product strategy process structure. It provides the foundation for product strategy, especially in companies that have multiple products related by common technology. Product platforms define the cost structure, capabilities, and differentiation of subsequent products. By separating product platform strategy from product line and individual product strategy, a company can better concentrate its focus on strategic issues.

A product platform is a concept for product planning and strategic decision making. It is a collection of *common* technical elements, especially the underlying core technology, implemented across a range of products. These common elements are not necessarily complete in the sense that they are something that could be sold to a customer. They do, however, define the performance against customer requirements and the life cycle of the products that emanate from the platform.

The nature of product platforms varies widely across industries and product applications. For example, the product platform for a personal computer is its microprocessor combined with its operating system, such as the Apple Macintosh, Intel/Windows, or Digital Alpha/Windows NT platforms. The packaging, power supply, computer memory, disk drives, monitors, application software, and interface capabilities are all technical elements related to specific products, but they are not the focus of the product platform.

In spite of its importance, many companies tend to skip this critical level of product strategy and go directly to product line strategy. Some even skip that level too and go directly to the development of specific products. Eventually, they look back and realize that they developed the elements of a new product platform as part of one of these products, and then say, "If only we had thought of subsequent products before we completed these platform elements." Or even worse, they may forget to invest in developing the elements of a new product platform before their current one becomes obsolete, and then say, "We were caught off guard by the change in the market or technology."

Product platform strategy can best be represented in the form of an aggregate product platform plan. This shows the expected life cycle of all current product platforms and the anticipated schedule for new platforms. It shows where there may be serious gaps between product platforms and when development of new product platforms must begin. Implemented correctly, the process that creates this aggregate product platform plan forces companies to start the development of defining technical elements in advance.

Figure 7–2 illustrates an aggregate product platform plan.[1] It shows three different product platforms. Each illustrates a different product platform strategy situation. The plan shows both current and planned product platforms, with the dashed line distinguishing the past from the planned.

The high-performance systems product platform E-Comp is approaching the peak of its life cycle, and a product platform extension is planned to lengthen its competitive life. The strategy is to replace E-Comp with a new high-performance product platform, N/C-13, which uses an entirely different architecture. The extension of E-Comp is necessary since the technology for the new platform will not be available in time to prevent a gap between the two.

The mid-range systems platform, ESP, illustrates a derivative product platform, the ESP-Port. This product platform is similar to the ESP, but sufficiently different for the company to manage it as a distinctly different product platform. It is also at an earlier stage in its life cycle. The company has not yet decided on a next-generation replacement to its mid-range systems product platform. Through its product strategy process, the company identified this as an open issue and initiated a project to address it. Since the next-generation product platform is not defined, it is flagged with a question mark. The company plans to initiate development within a year.

The lowest portion of the aggregate product platform plan shows the platform strategy for a new market opportunity. In this case, the company has decided to enter this new market but is still unsure of the specific product platform for its new products. There are three very different product platforms being researched and evaluated: the Adv-P1, the SQ-II, and the HT-Ext. As the plan illustrates, the company will select one of these in the next few months as the product platform for the new market entry.

Product platform strategy should be the primary strategic focus for product strategy. Product platform decisions often turn out to be crucial to a company's growth and success. Together with the product strategy vision, product platform plans need to be integrated with a company's long-range strategic business planning process and should be the primary focus of top management attention with regard to product development.

Product platform strategy serves several essential purposes that affect the resulting product line, long-term business strategy, and technology strategy:

1. *It articulates market requirements and the intended vector of differentiation.* The products that emanate from the product platform will be successful only if there is a clear marketplace charter. Product platform strategy

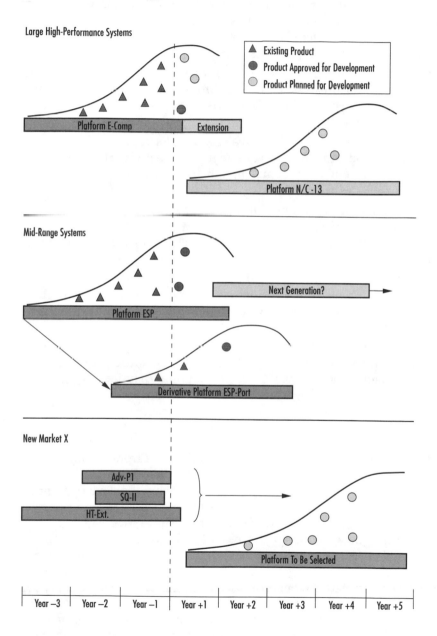

FIGURE 7–2 Illustrative aggregate product platform plan, showing the five-year outlook for multiple product platforms.

captures this charter in the form of key customer performance characteristics necessary to compete effectively in a market.

2. *It validates the current product platform life-cycle expectations.* New generations of products stem from new product platforms, not individual products. The life cycle of a product platform usually ends when it is replaced by a new, more competitive product platform, and a new product platform usually introduces a new generation of products.

3. *It determines whether a product platform should be extended.* The life of a product platform can be extended through periodic improvements. Personal computers illustrate this characteristic by using increased microprocessor speed to improve performance.

4. *It determines whether a derivative product platform should be developed.* A derivative product platform is one that is based primarily on an existing product platform, but is different enough to be managed as a separate product platform.

5. *It triggers the need for a modified product strategy vision.* While the product strategy vision typically does not change every year, there is a need to systematically identify major market and technology changes that might trigger such a change.

6. *It refines the current product line plan.* As markets evolve, products originally expected to be derived from a product platform might be dropped or changed. New segments may need to be addressed. Product development timing might be shifted. This is the mechanism for adjusting the cadence and substance of the product line plan.

7. *It triggers advanced technology development.* In anticipation of product platform development, product platform planning may identify areas of focus for new product technology, new distribution technology, new manufacturing technology, and so on. This provides important direction for R&D and other core business functions.

Product platform development is distinctly different from product development. Unlike product development, the goal is not directly to develop a new product, but to create the pieces or elements that enable the development of subsequent products. This difference in goals leads to differences in investment criteria, planning, and actual development.

Investments in new product platforms cannot be justified by the planned success of a single product, but rather need to be evaluated based on the expected success of all the resulting products from that platform. Financial evaluation of new product platform opportunities is done at a strategic level, using assumptions on the success of the resulting products. Some companies confuse product platform development with development of the initial product and are surprised when this first product is not financially justified. They either justify it as strategic and ignore the financial evaluation, or they discard it, possibly missing long-term opportunities.

Two or more product platforms can be integrated by use of common platform elements, such as components or modules. This increases leverage of expensive investments in technology even further. IBM illustrates this with its AS/400 and RS/6000 platforms. Both use the same microprocessor, the Power PC AS, but the AS/400-specific storage and memory-locking instructions are disabled in the RS/6000. The two platforms also share common memory subsystems, power supplies, and I/O controllers. However, each platform continues to keep separate software environments to maintain compatibility with its previous platform generations.[2]

A product platform development plan is different from a product development plan. It defines the common technical elements of a new product platform and how they will be developed. A product platform is completed when these common elements are ready to be incorporated into the lead product and subsequent products.

The process phases of product platform development are similar to the phases in product development that were described in Chapter 3, but there are some important differences:

- *Product platform concept evaluation* — This initial phase of product platform development defines the objectives and scope of the product platform, not a specific product. This includes an evaluation of the feasibility of the product platform and the expected products based on it, comparing alternative platforms that would accomplish the same objective. A company may put several alternative product platform concepts through this phase — either sequentially or in parallel — in order to select the best one. The decision to select a particular alternative and proceed with the next phase is the major decision of product platform strategy.
- *Product platform planning* — Detailed product platform planning that takes place during this next phase includes specification of the product platform's scope and its elements. This is where the common elements of the product platform are distinguished from the elements that are unique to individual products expected from this product platform. The detailed plan for the subsequent product platform development phase is also prepared at this time.
- *Product platform development* — The actual development of the platform elements takes place during this phase. These are passed on to the development project for the lead product, depending on a number of factors involving the readiness of technology, the timing of the lead product, and the need to develop these elements as part of a specific product program.

The phase review decisions for product platform development are also similar, but differ in a few important ways. The questions to be answered at the end of each phase are more strategic, covering a longer-term perspective for multiple products expected from the platform. Since the decisions are more strategic, they are sometimes made by a higher level of management.

Product platform development is also different from technology development. In its broadest sense, technology is a skill, capability, or core competency. Technology development can then be defined as creating or enabling this competency. Chapter 8 develops this distinction in more detail.

Product Line Strategy

Product line strategy is an integral aspect of product platform strategy, but in relative terms it is less critical. The product platform elements have already been selected. The primary basis of differentiation has been decided. The general cost structure has been determined. A brilliant product line strategy is unlikely to save an inept product platform strategy.

Nonetheless, product line strategy plays a crucial role in product strategy. A poorly implemented product line strategy can restrict the success of any platform strategy. Without product line strategy, companies fail to develop and release products in the proper sequence. They miss opportunities, and out of frustration try to do everything at once, only to find that they do not have sufficient resources.

Product line strategy is a time-phased conditional plan for the sequence of developing products within a product line. There are several important elements in this definition. It determines the *sequence* in which products are developed and released. This sequence is *time-phased* throughout the life cycle of the platform and the product line. Finally, it is *conditional*. It can change based on a better understanding of the market, competitive factors, or resource availability.

The evolution of Apple's Macintosh product line presents an interesting illustration of how a product line evolves (see Figure 7–3).[3] The Apple Lisa was the forerunner of the Macintosh product line. Lisa used the 32-bit Motorola 68000 microprocessor, user interface, and graphics capabilities that evolved into the Macintosh. After Lisa was introduced with a lot of fanfare in mid-1983, however, its weaknesses became apparent. Even though Lisa used a 32-bit microprocessor, it was slower than the IBM PC because its extensive graphics capability consumed so much of the higher processing power. At $10,000 it proved to be too expensive. Additionally, it lacked sufficient software and couldn't be networked. As a result of these failings, Lisa sales dropped precipitously three months after introduction, leaving Apple with capacity that far exceeded demand.

The Macintosh was introduced in January of 1984 at a price of $2,495. It used the Motorola 68000 microprocessor, but also introduced the 3 1/2-inch disk drive. The drive was made for Apple by Sony, who had first introduced the drive two years earlier in its unsuccessful entry into the personal computer

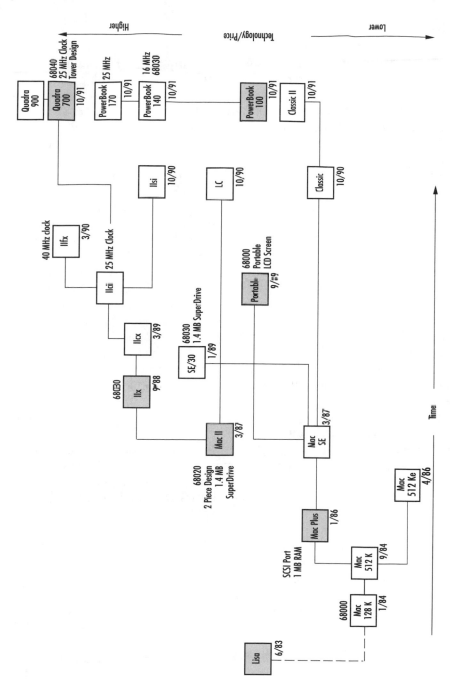

FIGURE 7–3   Apple Macintosh product line.

market. (Sony sold only 1,600 computers in the U.S. before the product was withdrawn.)

The Macintosh was an immediate success. Apple sold 50,000 in the first seventy-four days. Initial problems due to its limited 128-KB memory were overcome when the 512-KB version was introduced in September 1984, four months earlier than expected. By the end of 1984, however, sales of the Macintosh began to slow. Apple was selling only approximately 20,000 units per month, when it had been expecting to sell between 60,000 and 85,000.[4]

At the beginning of 1986, the Macintosh Plus was introduced. It included cursor keys and a numeric keypad for spreadsheet users as well as internal memory expandability to 1 million bytes. Fortunately for Apple, Microsoft had just released Excel for the Macintosh.

In March of 1987, Apple introduced the second Macintosh generation: the Macintosh II and the Macintosh SE (system expansion). The Macintosh II was an open design for advanced applications with a built-in hard disk, color display, and network connections. Work had actually started on this product back in 1984. The Macintosh SE included additional internal memory and an internal slot for additional functions. It was specifically targeted at business users. Apple saw the development of these products as a race against the introduction of the new IBM PS/2 product line (which they beat by a month).

Apple has introduced many variations of the original Macintosh II, including the IIx and IIfx, which were not successful. The IIfx was a high-priced product that sold less than 36,000 units in its first year.[5] Apple's entry into the portable market was also less than successful. The 14-pound Mac Portable sold less than half of the number of units expected.

The low end of the market has proved to be a good segment for the Macintosh. The Mac Classic, an entry-level product at $995, was a big success, exceeding everyone's expectations. Interestingly, Apple considered a low-cost Macintosh back in 1984. But instead of expanding its product line at the low end, it opted for expanding into the higher-performance, higher-margin segments. The Macintosh product line could have been much more successful with earlier expansion into the low end.

In October of 1991, Apple launched a number of new products, including a higher-performance Classic; the Classic II; its first notebook computer, the PowerBook; and a new high-performance line, the Quadra. The PowerBook was designed for Apple primarily by engineers at Sony. They were able to complete this project in thirteen months from a half-page specification.[6] The PowerBook 100 weighed five pounds, had two megabytes of memory and was priced at $2,300. The PowerBook 140 and PowerBook 170 were more powerful versions of the same product.

The Macintosh product line plan shows how specific products were designed for different market segments using the same product platform elements, the microprocessor and operating system. The Macintosh II product family addressed the changing needs of high-performance user segments through 1990 until the new Quadra line was introduced. The Mac Plus product family, on the other hand, addressed lower-performance market segments, including educators, personal desktop users, and small offices/home offices. In the early 90s, a new market segment emerged — the portable segment, with its own spectrum of high-performance versus low-performance segments. The PowerBook product family addressed the needs of this critical new segment. Apple addressed the needs of these three segments with three separate product families based on a common product platform: the Macintosh operating system and Motorola 68000 microprocessor.

Expansion Strategy

Expansion into totally new product lines can be the most exciting type of product strategy. This is usually how companies grow rapidly and is what is traditionally viewed as innovation. Identifying the best opportunities for new product lines is also the most difficult function of product strategy, since the potential opportunities are vast and the risks are high.

A new product platform and resulting product line is more likely to be successful when it leverages a company's existing strengths in marketing and technology. By leveraging its strengths, a company creates advantages to offset the challenges of a new product line. Conversely, history has shown a high failure rate for new product lines without this leverage. In spite of this, many companies attempt new product lines without much planning or forethought.

The framework in Figure 7–4 helps companies target opportunities for innovating new product lines. It positions new product line opportunities on two dimensions: product technology and market/distribution channel. The product-technology dimension ranges from the same product to similar products, to the same or similar technology, to completely new technology. The market dimension ranges from the same market and distribution channel, to new markets through the same distribution channel, to completely new markets and distribution channels.

Current product lines are positioned in Figure 7–4 as the starting point in the lower left-hand corner. From there a company can move in three directions to introduce new product lines. The usual boundaries for success in these directions are shown by the shaded area. Beyond these boundaries a company loses the benefit of leveraging its experience.

Texas Instruments (TI) illustrates some good examples of this framework. In 1975, as calculators were becoming commodity items, TI looked for new opportunities to apply its technology. TI initially targeted the increased use of calculators in the classroom environment and developed a product that included a calculator and also a math instruction book that was aimed at improving classroom learning. The company marketed this package directly to school systems — an example of a very similar product sold to a

114   *Setting the PACE in Product Development*

completely new market through a new distribution channel, one that was outside TI's expertise. Within the framework shown in Figure 7–4, this effort went beyond the lightly shaded boundary and was a clear failure.

Following this, however, TI pursued a more targeted approach and identified a similar product need for a new market (children learning math) through its existing distribution channels (consumer electronics stores). The Little Professor was an electronic flash card, a calculator in reverse. It presented the problem and the child provided the answer. Introduced in August 1976 for under $20, the Little Professor was tremendously successful. TI could not make enough of them for the 1976 Christmas season. TI expanded the Little Professor product line with products like Dataman in 1977.

TI subsequently targeted a new product line that leveraged the Little Professor by introducing a new product aimed at the same market but that also introduced new technology — speech synthesis. The TI Speak and Spell, for example, a talking device that helped children learn how to spell, came out in

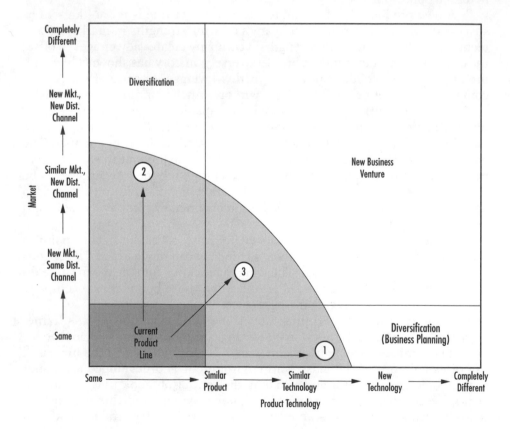

FIGURE 7–4   Framework for expansion into new markets.

mid-1978. It was also tremendously successful. TI has continued to build and expand this product line.

Using the framework in Figure 7–4, a company can look for new product line/platform opportunities in three primary directions. Each of these leverages different strengths and offers different opportunities.

1. *Similar/new technologies and same market/distribution channel.* Targeting a new product line using these parameters has been a successful method of expansion for many companies. This form of innovation can be customer or technology driven.

Eastman Kodak used its skills in digital graphics to partially change a mature market where it had a strong customer base: 35mm photography. In 1992, it introduced the photo CD player, which stored 100 photos on a CD prepared by local photo finishers. In addition to having a consumer market, the photo CD could be a tool for businesses such as real estate firms and retailers, creating the opportunity for Kodak to expand into a directly related market at the same time.

In the consumer products industry, the Swiss Corporation for Microelectronics and Watchmaking Industries (Swatch) realized that it had saturated the watch market and looked to related products for the same market. It leveraged its skills in designing products that are fun and easy to use, and combined this with relatively simple telecommunications technology to develop the Swatch Twinphone. This unique product enables two people to use the phone at the same time. It targets the same type of customer who buys Swatch watches and is sold through the same distribution channels. New product line innovation targeted at this same market includes a pager-watch.

2. *Similar product and new market/distribution channel.* Expanding into new markets or distribution channels based on an existing product platform usually requires some product variation, but the emphasis is on new markets. Several examples illustrate this.

Microsoft introduced the Excel spreadsheet for the Macintosh in May 1985. By 1987, it had captured 89% of the Macintosh spreadsheet market.[7] A version of Excel for the IBM PC market was an obvious new product opportunity and development began shortly after the Macintosh version was released. In October 1987, the PC version of Excel was released. This provides an example of a similar product developed for a different but related market.

Sun Microsystems has adapted its computer operating system to run on other computers. Scott McNealy, Sun's president, believes that "Sun is sitting on a huge market opportunity." It is taking a similar product, its SunOS operating system, adapting it, and selling it into an entirely new market: other microcomputers. When looked at as a separate market, Sun sold approximately 150,000 operating systems in 1990 compared to 5.2 million Microsoft MS-DOS and 333,000 IBM OS/2 systems. For Sun this is a new market that clearly requires a new channel of distribution, since it is selling operating systems to run on other computers.[8]

AutoDesk scaled down its very successful AutoCAD computer-aided design software to run on personal computers at a lower price. It aimed AutoCAD LT at a related market: architects, designers, and engineers who needed a design tool that did not require more advanced features or development tools. The goal of AutoCAD LT was to increase revenue by expansion into a related market.

3. *Combining similar/new technologies and related markets.* The most fertile area for expansion is based on a combination of similar and new product technology for new markets, using the same distribution channel. This expansion strategy leverages both technology and market experience to create new markets. We have already seen an example of this in the TI Little Professor. Another example is the successful expansion of companies into the VCR product line.

In the early 1970's, Matsushita, JVC, and Sony began expanding into the consumer market for video cassette recorders. They did this by leveraging their success in television and audio products while perfecting the new video recording technology originally developed by Ampex, RCA, and Toshiba for the broadcast industry. Matsushita, JVC, and Sony targeted a new market (those who wanted to tape television programs), using the same distribution channel (consumer electronics stores), and a combination of similar (consumer electronics) and new (videotape recording) technology. By 1983, these three companies had almost 60% of a nearly 20-million-unit market.

Ironically, Ampex squandered its leading-edge capabilities in magnetic video recording by trying to expand into computer peripherals and consumer audio — areas that lie in the much riskier new-business-venture region on the framework shown in Figure 7–4.

EMC Corporation was moderately successful building add-on memory boards for large computers. In 1988, it decided to build on its skills and expand into data storage systems. This was a directly related market that required a totally new platform. EMC's storage system platform was designed using many small disk drives strung together to create a large, efficient data storage capacity. This new platform was tremendously successful, and EMC expanded to become one of the fastest-growing companies in the U.S., achieving $780 million in revenue in 1993.

This framework helps identify specific new product opportunities through specific questions. How can a similar product be applied to a new market? What new markets can be reached through current distribution channels? How can the technology in the existing product be applied to similar products?

At the same time, the framework keeps companies from making mistakes. One company that wanted to expand into a new market initiated development in the totally unrelated areas of diversification and new business ventures (the unshaded regions in Figure 7–4). These efforts involved both new technology and new channels of distribution at the same time. The expansion efforts failed while the company's competitors expanded with new, but related, products into the same, or related, markets. After understanding this framework, the company terminated its initial expansion and looked for new opportunities in related products within existing distribution channels.

Where does expansion strategy fit into the product strategy process? The answer lies in the top two elements of the process structure: product strategy vision and product platform strategy. In developing the product strategy vision, there must be an assessment of that vision's ability to meet business growth goals. When growth goals cannot be met with the current and planned product lines based on existing product platforms, this gap triggers the need for expansion strategy. Alternatively, product platform strategy might identify an under-leveraged product platform, one that could be expanded to support a broader array of products. Both the product strategy vision and the product platform strategy can provide the impetus for expansion into new markets.

Competitive Strategy Skills

A company can have an adequate process for product strategy in place, but without skillful execution, it still may not develop a successful strategy. Skillful execution begins with a conceptual understanding of competitive product strategy. The following competitive strategy concepts illustrate the skills needed:[9]

- *Product differentiation* — Product differentiation is the preferred competitive strategy of high-technology companies. When successfully differentiated, a product can command a premium price because it provides a higher added value to customers. Differentiation positions products competitively in a market and segments the market based on customer preferences.

    Differentiation is best achieved through vectors instead of individual points, such as a new feature. Vectors of differentiation establish, and progressively improve, a consistent theme of differentiation, such as ease of use. This raises differentiation to a strategic-level rather than a design-level decision.
- *Price-based strategy* — The secondary strategy for competitively positioning products is price based. All companies have a price-based strategy, but most ignore it as a product strategy. Instead they manage it tactically, suffering strategic consequences as a result. Price-based strategies can be offensive or defensive. Offensive price-based strategies require a company to exploit all sources of cost advantage.
- *Time-based strategy* — Time-based strategy is a supporting competitive strategy. It is becoming increasingly popular because it creates an advantage by being the first or the fastest. These advantages lead to two types of time-based strategy: first-to-market or fast-follower.

- *Global product strategy* — For many high-technology products, the economic advantage of a global product strategy can be so significant that it can completely overshadow products from local or regional competitors. This advantage emphasizes the importance of globalization in product strategy. However, there are many reasons why products are difficult to globalize.
- *Cannibalization strategy* — Cannibalization is a recurrent strategic issue, particularly for high-technology companies, as emerging technology drives them to continuously upgrade and replace their existing products. Cannibalization is a controversial strategic issue that comes into play when a company's new product will be successful at the expense of another of its own products. In some cases, cannibalization should be avoided; in other cases, avoiding it encourages competitive attack.

Why Companies Have Problems Developing Product Strategy

Very few companies are comfortable with the way they develop product strategy. The primary underlying reason is that they don't manage product strategy as a process and the following problems result:

- They focus on individual products instead of product platforms.
- They don't anticipate the end-of-platform life cycles.
- New product opportunities arise sporadically.
- Opportunities for expansion are not deliberately explored.
- Product strategy is done only as part of annual budgeting.

References

1. This example is from Michael E. McGrath, *Product Strategy for High-Technology Companies* (Burr Ridge, Ill.: Irwin Professional Publishing, 1995). Reproduced by permission.

2. Jean S. Bozman and Craig Stedman, "AS/400, RS/6000 to Share Power PC Chip," *Computerworld* (December 11, 1995).

3. For a description of product line mapping, see Steven C. Wheelwright and W. Earl Sasser, Jr., "The New Product Development Map," *Harvard Business Review* (May–June 1989).

4. John Sculley, *Odyssey* (New York: Harper & Row, 1989), 230.

5. *Upside* (October 1991): 38.

6. *Fortune* (November 4, 1991): 151.

7. Daniel Ichbiah and Susan L. Knepper, *The Making of Microsoft* (Rocklin, Calif.: Prima Publishing, 1991), 169.

8. *Business Week* (September 9, 1991): 87.

9. For a detailed description of these competitive strategies, see Michael E. McGrath, *Product Strategy for High-Technology Companies*.

CHAPTER 8

Technology Management

Emmett W. Eldred
Amram R. Shapiro

Imagine that every time you developed a product, the technologies that you needed were sitting on a shelf, like modular building blocks needing only to be selected and integrated with each other. Imagine that these were the best technologies, state-of-the-art, fully tested and debugged. Moreover, they were proprietary, well protected by patents, trade secrecy, and applications know-how only you fully possessed. In short, imagine that technical uncertainty had been reduced to a bare minimum, to issues of how well you exploit your technology position, not whether it will do what is needed or whether competitors may have better technology. What would be the impact of this dream condition on your development success rate and cycle time?

A major element of risk would have been eliminated from the development of product strategy. You could select the right combinations of product performance, features, and cost to maximize your market share and return. Product line planning would be a matter of spacing out your winners and managing the pace of advance. Cycle times would be short despite high degrees of innovation, with the key issue being time-efficient execution. Product introductions would be highly predictable and the allocation of development resources would be easily optimized.

This is, of course, a pleasant fantasy, not a state that can be achieved. Technology uncertainty and risk are inescapable. They can't be made to disappear; they can only be managed. The point of this daydream is that achieving even modest improvements in technology management can yield enormous benefits.

Technology development can have a significant impact on time-to-market. When development times are too long, a root cause is often incomplete technology development. Sometimes the problem is transferring the technology. Just because the research lab knows how to make a technology work in a laboratory environment doesn't mean that product developers can easily apply it. Sometimes the technology is not developed enough to transfer. Properly scoping a product concept is very difficult when one of the defining technologies it incorporates is not well reduced to practice. If extensive invention is done concurrently with product development, the uncertain timing of the former makes scheduling very difficult. The risks and uncertainties imposed by an untried technology tend to stretch out management decision making.

In this chapter, we describe how technology is best managed to achieve Product And Cycle-time Excellence. We will begin with a look at the differences between technology and product development and then briefly review the four main challenges in technology management. These are:

- *Technology development* — how to best manage the process of developing specific newly identified or sought for "sensed technologies"
- *Technology transfer* — how to move technology into product development and commercialization
- *Technology strategy* — how to determine what core technologies to work on in support of product and business strategy
- *Technology infrastructure* — how to maintain the skills and facilities to support technology strategy

Technology Development Differs from Product Development

Effective technology management begins with understanding the differences between technology development and product development. This understanding improves communication between scientists and general managers, and transfers between technology development and product development teams.

Unlike product development, the ultimate outcome of a technology development effort is unpredictable. Technology programs are often breaking new ground, so it is difficult to predict how long they will take. Planned completion dates for technical development tasks are more goals than reliable commitments.

Some other distinctive characteristics of technology development programs include:

- The network of possible experimental outcomes is so vast that detailed overall project planning is impractical.
- Determining when a technology is ready for product development can seem very subjective and hard to agree on.
- Too much structure can inhibit creativity.
- It is difficult to capture process experience and leverage it for future technology development efforts.

One way to visualize the difference between technology and product development is to use the metaphor of a series of walls, each containing a door through which the researcher or developer must pass as the program proceeds.

Product development walls are depicted as transparent in Figure 8–1, using the PACE phases described in Chapter 3. A developer can usually see through the walls to the final product release almost from the start of the product development process. It is through the capture and leveraging of development experience that the product development walls become transparent. With structured product development and cycle-time metrics, reasonably accurate projections for each phase can be set in advance.

Technology development walls, representing major technical milestones, are opaque (see Figure 8–2). Technology development programs often break new ground and the nature of the coming milestone is not usually known until the previous one is reached. There may be a fairly clear understanding of the number of walls (that is, the overall technical development plan) and the ultimate objective (defined technical objectives); however, the specific experimental approach for activities between each wall is not known to the research team until it passes through the door and can view the next technical challenge, the next opaque wall. How long it will take to get through these walls is very hard to estimate in advance.

Technology development is much more unpredictable than product development. Prematurely introducing "unfinished" technology into the product development process leads to schedule uncertainty, unexpected slippages, and, often, to project failure. Because of this, technology development programs

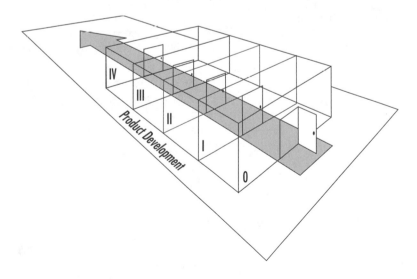

FIGURE 8–1   Product development "walls."

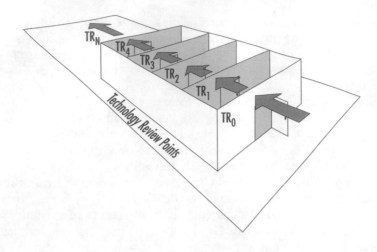

FIGURE 8–2   Technology development "walls."

must be run differently from product development programs, and the process of technology transfer into product development is critical.

Technology Development

Sometimes senior business managers abdicate the responsibility for managing technology projects to researchers in the hope that the researchers will inform them when the "time is right." This approach does not usually work effectively. Given how hard it is to understand and communicate when the time *is* right, both researchers and business managers have searched for an approach that works better. What they seek is a structured process appropriate to technology development, distinct from but linked to the product development process, in which both business and scientific management collaborate.

What follows is a description of the key components of the PACE technology development process. Through the balance and integration of these components, technology can be developed efficiently for use in product development.

Technology Review Process

As in the Phase Review Process described in Chapter 3, the Technology Review Process provides the primary framework for technology development, but with some important differences. The Technology Review Process consists of a series of pre-set reviews of project progress at the end of each development phase. This is illustrated in Figure 8–3. As a technology development program progresses from one technology review to the next, technical alternatives are narrowed down, uncertainty decreases, and there is an overall increase in technical understanding. At each of these reviews, senior management decides whether the program should move to the next phase, be redirected, or be canceled. The Technology Review Process has several characteristics:

- It is divided into a series of technology review phases (referred to as phases TR^0 through TR^N). Each of these technology reviews represents a significant technical milestone and a key evaluation point.
- Collectively, the number and sequence of the phases represent the overall technology development plan. Because development approach and timeframe vary for different technologies, the phases will vary in number from one program to another.
- A technology development program begins with the identification of a single "sensed technology" or set of "sensed technologies" to be the focus of the program. Sensed technology can take several forms. For example, it can be a newly discovered technology with yet-undefined product application, such as Polymerase Chain Reaction (PCR) for replicating target DNA strands, or it can be a list of desired technical performance criteria for future products, for which technology is needed. In any case, sensed technology represents the starting point for a technology development effort.
- The first phase of the technology development program includes agreement on the program objectives and the overall development plan (number and definition of phases).
- Each technology review provides a period for enabling a technology and evaluating it against program objectives.
- Because of the uncertainty about the experimental focus of later phases, detailed plans are only appropriate for the upcoming phase. A fairly accurate

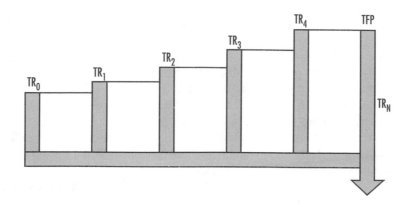

FIGURE 8–3   Technology Review Process.

prediction of the number of phases and what each phase represents is usually possible. An estimate of program duration can be made based on the assumptions built into the technology development plan and revisited at each technology phase review.

- Confidence in the technology's potential grows as the program passes through successive phases.

Technology Feasibility Point

To know when a technology development program has made enough progress to have a technology in hand ready to be applied in products, there needs to be a clear definition of the technology confidence level. At some point, technical uncertainty or risk remaining in a program is small or controllable enough that it can be addressed during product development. This is called the technology feasibility point (TFP), the agreed-upon confidence level that defines the end of a technology development program at TR^N. It is expressed as a matrix of experimental outcomes (based on the more general technical performance criteria targets) that, if met, collectively provide adequate confidence that the remaining technology optimization can be completed during the normal course of the ensuing product development effort.

For example, a medical consumables company identified an opportunity for disposable, one-time applicators. It determined that the development of an organic material capable of swelling to two times its original volume upon brief exposure to alcohol would provide a core technology enabling the development of a new product platform. Because of market timing and competitive pressures, this TFP was intentionally set low and, once reached, still represented a substantial technical risk.

Once the TFP is reached, other technical alternatives are typically ruled out, and the drive toward a specific product begins. It is also at this point that a clearer definition of the final product (functional specification) can be more accurately estimated.

Figure 8–4 illustrates three differing rates of technology development from the point of a sensed technology to the defined TFP. Vector A progresses faster than B, while C wanders without ever reaching the TFP. The goal of technology management is to ensure that programs such as A and B reach their objectives as quickly as possible, while programs such as C do not continue to absorb valuable developmental resources indefinitely.

The final phase (TR^N) of the Technology Review Process is focused on integrating the technology into specific product platforms and product development programs. Approval to enter this final phase means that a technology is considered ready for transfer into an upcoming product. The TFP has been attained. Completion of phase TR^N means that the product development effort has been initiated, and a transition team has been formed that is responsible for carrying the technology forward.

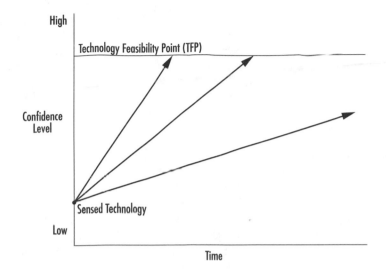

High

Technology Feasibility Point (TFP)

Confidence
Level

Sensed Technology

Low

Time

FIGURE 8–4   Comparison of three programs' rate of progress to TFP.

Senior Review Committee

The Senior Review Committee (SRC) is a decision-making body of senior sci
entists and business managers that oversee technology development projects
via technology phase reviews. It has the authority to fund and prioritize technology development programs. The business managers represent the operating
units that will commercialize the technology, while the senior scientists represent R&D management. Depending on the phase or nature of the technology
development project, other technical or business advisors or consultants are in-
vited to participate on the SRC.

The SRC combines a scientific and a business perspective at technology
reviews. These reviews are usually divided into two parts: the first is a scientific peer review, and the second focuses on the business or investment aspects
of the project. During the first part, SRC senior scientists and technical advisors evaluate the program from a scientific point of view, reviewing both the
conclusions reached during the prior phase and the experimental plans for the
upcoming phase. They focus especially on the quality of science and the team's
evaluation of the technology's proximity to the TFP. The business members of
the SRC can participate in this initial session, but often leave the detailed scientific discussions to the researchers. The second part of the phase review involves attaining understanding and agreement among members of the SRC
about how far the technology has progressed toward being ready for application
in product development (the technology confidence level).

At each phase review, the SRC empowers the technology development team and approves necessary resources. Based on the technology development team's recommendation, the SRC decides whether to approve, redirect, or cancel the program's progression into the next phase. It is the SRC's responsibility to make the final assessment of the confidence levels attained and to determine when a TFP has been reached.

Structured Development Process

A structured process applied to technology development provides a framework for project planning and execution. It improves communication, conveys a sense of urgency and business purpose, and reduces wasted research expenditure.

The structured development process for technology is hierarchical, with detail increasing as one moves to the base of the pyramid. There are four levels, as shown in Figure 8–5: technology development plans, individual phase plans, experiments, and laboratory activities.

At the top of the pyramid is the technology development plan. It represents an overview of the entire technology development program, broken down by phase and condensed onto one page. Since the number or duration of individual phases can often only be estimated, the technology development plan provides an outline for the overall program. It is a "best guess" as to the most efficient approach to enabling and evaluating the targeted underlying technology.

The next level of detail is that of the individual phase plan. This is a flowchart of the integrated experiments within each phase. It is based on informa-

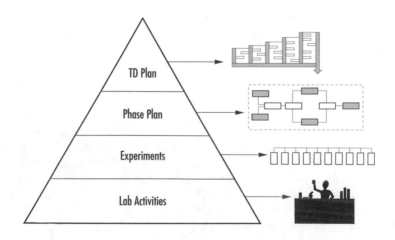

FIGURE 8–5   The structured development hierarchy for technology.

tion gained from previous phases and defines the approach needed to reach the next major technical milestone. This flowchart format provides researchers with adequate structure to plan concurrent experimental activities (highlighting key dependencies or chronological linkages), while maintaining enough simplicity and flexibility to not dampen creativity. It also provides the primary management tool for the technology development team leader to orchestrate the team's activities during the phase.

The greatest level of detail, actual experimental design and specific laboratory activities, are planned at the laboratory level. Prior to each phase review, senior SRC scientists might request that the design or results of a key experiment be included in the phase review.

Technology Transfer: Linking Technology Development to Product Development

The objective of the technology development process is to build sufficient confidence in a technology that a product development program is initiated. Phase TR^N of the Technology Review Process is where the transfer takes place.

Senior technical and business managers routinely underestimate the time and effort required to transfer a new technology into product development. Some feel that having researchers document their work and meet with a product development team is enough. Many project retrospectives have shown that this is rarely the case. Both sides of the transfer are often dissatisfied. Product developers may complain that the technology development team didn't do enough to evaluate and enable the technology, while researchers may feel that the product development team didn't do enough to understand the incoming technology or were somehow trying to "reinvent the wheel." Because technology and product development have such different goals, approaches, and structures, there needs to be an effective technology transfer process that bridges the technology and product development processes.

Program Synchronization

A product development effort begins with a product concept formulated by a champion or a concept team. In either case, technology team members should participate in the formulation of the product concept. This is when technology development and product development are synchronized.

It is important to have a fairly clear product concept prior to the initiation of the transfer process. Otherwise, the technical transition team members will be forced to either halt work while a concept is finalized or continue working without a clear understanding of specific customer or market needs. When the latter occurs, R&D may charge ahead, creating its own interpretation of a product concept. If concept decisions continue to be delayed, the

R&D alternative may become the only viable one by default, if it is seen as the only way to achieve the desired time-to-market.

Technology Equalization

A product development project relies on many technologies. Some are core technologies, those that define the innovation. Others are supporting technologies, necessary to the product, though perhaps not so differentiating. Core technologies tend to get most of the attention. They are likely to be the technologies that are transferred, having reached their TFP in TR^N. During technology equalization, the supporting technologies that must reach similar confidence levels are identified and their TFPs set.

Technology equalization is especially vital when combining science and engineering in the ultimate product. For example, if a new core chemistry has been developed for an analytical procedure, it can be commercially applied in products that are manual, semi-automated, or automated. During technology development, the enabling and evaluating effort would have focused primarily on the performance characteristics of the chemistry relative to its intended use in the analytical protocol. However, as the chemistry moves from technology development into product development, other technologies become important, depending on the desired final product. In the case of an automated system, there would be numerous other technical considerations, such as auto-calibration or automated sample handling and processing, while a manual assay test format would require simpler supporting technologies.

The technology equalization process is represented in Figure 8–6. The Y axis represents the confidence in the technology. The X axis represents the various technological factors. The TFP line represents an agreed-upon confidence level, which when reached provides adequate confidence that the remaining technical optimization can be completed during the normal course of the ensuing product development effort.

The technology equalization process initially involves surveying all technical aspects of a new product (unbundling), and then prioritizing these technical components based on their overall importance (chronologically and relationally) and their confidence level. Once this prioritization has been done, workplans focused on enabling and evaluating key technical components can be constructed, and the critical path identified. In this way, the information required will be available prior to the key decision points. Since management will better understand the trade-offs between risk and time-to-market, it will be able to make better trade-off decisions.

Usually, the technology equalization process is initiated at the final phase (TR^N) of the technology development process and at the earliest phase (product concept) of product development. It continues through the planning and functional specification phase and is a critical component in helping design the integrated project development plan, including identification of key technical or design review points.

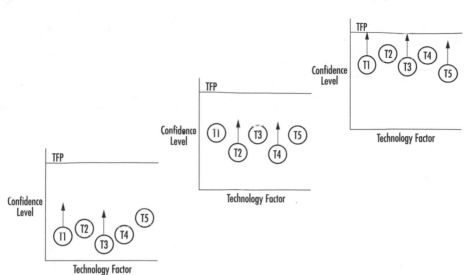

FIGURE 8–6   Technology equalization.

Technology Transition Teams

Since technology transfer often requires the coordination of people with very different perspectives (for example, research scientists and marketers), and may be quite complex logistically, a structured process with clearly defined roles and responsibilities is indispensable.

Central to the technology transfer process is the transition team. The transition team has evolving team membership, usually starting with key representatives from the technology development team and the newly forming product development Core Team. Additional members from other functions are added as necessary. The product development champion or future Core Team leader usually assumes the responsibility of transition team leader. The transition team ultimately evolves into the product development Core Team after the initial phase of product development.

The transition team puts together a high-level transition plan, which initially concentrates on the transition of the core technology into product development, and begins the process of technology equalization. The transition team identifies the supporting technologies and sets its TFPs. The program logistics must also be detailed in the plan.

The technology transfer plan is reviewed and decided on in a joint meeting of the SRC and the Product Approval Committee (PAC), which often have some overlapping membership. This joint meeting serves to initialize the technology transfer program. Subsequent reviews are conducted by the PAC through its Phase Review Process. The number of subsequent reviews depends on the nature of the project, but typically is closely tied to the key review points identified during the technology equalization process.

The transfer of developers to the Core Team for product development or to multiple Core Teams through a role in the outer "support team" ring is common. For simple instances of technology transfer (e.g., technology application from a divisional laboratory), the process may be facilitated by an individual researcher joining a concept Core Team.

Technology Strategy — Linking Technology Development to Product Strategy

The objective of a technology strategy is to address four questions in a concise and meaningful way:

1. *Which technologies are needed to support current product platforms?* Technology often extends the life of current platforms, buying time for a company to build its next. Understanding the remaining improvement in the technologies that the platform is built on is critical. This defines the remaining potential of the platform.

2. *Which technologies must be developed to support or enable new product platforms?* Where new product platforms have been identified, the challenge is to understand which technologies will be key and which will be supporting. Techniques such as technology unbundling are invaluable here to identify both.

3. *What is the potential of these technologies?* Some of the most critical questions to address are: How does the technology contribute to the chosen vector of differentiation? What is its maturity? How does it compare with competing technologies? How protectable is it from an intellectual property standpoint?

4. *How can practical access to the needed technologies be gained?* Technology strategy always includes a make-or-buy perspective. Given the rate of technological innovation and change, corporations cannot afford to assume that they alone will develop all that they need to build on. Keeping open the options of licensing or outright technology purchase provides alternatives to devoting scarce technical resources to every technology need.

There are many techniques, such as technology unbundling or the use of product/technology roadmaps, that can help answer these questions, but the key point is that technology strategy and product strategy are, practically speaking, hard to separate. New product platforms almost always rest on new technology platforms. And new technology platforms almost always imply the need to develop new product platforms to be well exploited commercially.

The strategic link between technology management and pipeline management is the focus of the next chapter. It addresses how technology development organizations maintain the skills and facilities needed to fulfill their mission.

As technology strategy defines the core technologies of focus, research management must ensure that the technical skills and tools are in place to deliver those technologies. Identifying the skills needed, finding people with them, and integrating them into research programs is one of the key skills of the research manager, and one of the most strategic, with long-term implications for technology development.

Why Companies Have Problems Managing Technology Development

Most companies don't feel that they do a very good job managing technology development, and they're right. Typical failings include:

- They don't have any defined process for technology development, leaving it up to each development group.
- Technology development decisions are not based on clearly defined expectations and criteria.
- The technology transfer process is undefined; in some cases, it's expected to just happen naturally.

CHAPTER 9

Pipeline Management

John R. Harris
Jonathan C. McKay

Project management effectiveness — Core Teams, Phase Review Process, structured methodology — allows companies to get *individual* products to market quickly and efficiently. However, competitive pressures are increasingly challenging companies to go beyond successful management at the project level and manage all their R&D investments as a group. This requires better management in balancing the mix of investments in product development.

In order to achieve this balance, companies have to manage their development pipeline to optimal levels of performance. They need to make more sophisticated resource allocation decisions that reflect the interrelationships of one project to another. They must concern themselves with not only the individual merits of a specific product opportunity but also how the overall mix of projects fits their product strategy vision. In addition, they need to integrate product development decisions more effectively into the functional budgets that are part of every company's business plan.

The symptoms of the need for better pipeline management are commonplace and include product strategies not based on realistic organizational capabilities and resources, functional budgets misaligned with project plans, organizational bottlenecks that consistently delay projects, lack of resources to staff projects as planned, chronic fire fighting, and so on. Pipeline management, as described in this chapter, addresses the underlying causes of these symptoms.

Individual techniques such as portfolio management have been employed in some cases to address these needs. However, these techniques focus on determining the best mix of products, not how the projects progress and interact through their development. They are usually done in "snapshot" form, solving the problem only temporarily. The biggest shortcoming of portfolio management is that it leaves unanswered the critical question: What specifically needs to be done to get the desired mix of projects to market?

Pipeline management links product strategy to project management and functional management, as shown in Figure 9–1, to optimally deploy a company's development-related resources (primarily people, but also critical equipment, support services, and so on).[1] This is accomplished through three activities that link together critical processes and functions:

- *Strategic balancing* sets priorities among numerous opportunities and adjusts the organization's capabilities to deliver new products.
- *Pipeline loading* fine-tunes resource deployment by adding additional visibility to the decisions made in the Phase Review Process.
- *Aligning functional delivery* ensures that functional managers maximize the flow of projects through the organization in both the short and long term.

All three activities must be in place and synchronized to avoid the common shortcoming in which each function and each project attempts to optimize its own performance, leading to sub-optimal overall product development performance.

The cadence of pipeline management differs among companies, depending on factors such as marketplace volatility, rate of technology change, typical

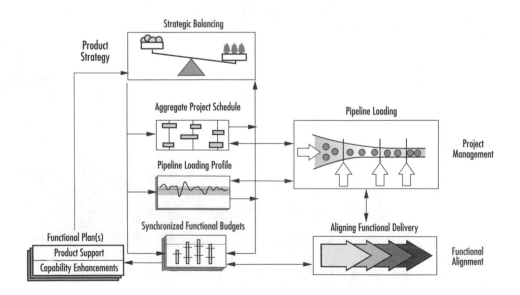

FIGURE 9–1   Pipeline management framework.

development cycle times, and so on. In most cases, companies are locked into sub-optimal performance because the cadence of their annual planning and budgeting cycle does not match the needs of effective pipeline management. For example, PC (personal computer) manufacturers face a market in which new PCs are introduced every six months, and should respond by adjusting their pipelines strategically every six months, on a project basis every two weeks, and functionally on a daily basis. Contrast this with pharmaceutical companies that have product development cycles of more than a decade and adjust their pipelines strategically every few years, project-wise on a semi-annual basis, and functionally every month.

Strategic Balancing

Effective pipeline management starts with the senior management team as it determines how it will strategically balance its development pipeline to realize its product strategies. Strategic balance is achieved by balancing the portfolio of development projects and related activities along many dimensions, such as focus versus diversification, short- versus long-term impact, high versus low risk, extending existing platforms versus development of new platforms, and so on. However, strategic balancing is different from traditional portfolio approaches, which can unfocus an organization by adding a "wish list" of product ideas to an already overloaded product development pipeline.

Strategic balancing tightly links product strategies[2] with organizational capabilities and capacities. It is an iterative process that results in the selection of development projects that are feasible and achieve organizational goals. Achieving strategic balance is not a trivial exercise. Companies performing strategic balancing for the first time are frequently astounded by the state of their product development pipeline. For example, a computer manufacturer analyzed its product development pipeline and found that the pipeline was 40% over capacity with just its existing development projects, before adding any new projects. Through strategic balancing, the company brought the pipeline back into balance and shifted its focus from short-term to long-term.

Strategic balancing sets empowerment boundaries for Product Approval Committee (PAC) decision making during phase reviews and for functional managers making resource deployment decisions. In this way, strategic balancing deploys product strategy without adding bureaucracy, through the use of an aggregate project schedule[3], a pipeline loading profile, and synchronized functional budgets.

- The *aggregate project schedule* is an optimized development master schedule. This time-sequenced, conditional map of desired projects is the embodiment of product strategy and thus is used during phase reviews as the context within which to charter and deploy resources to Core Teams. This schedule is updated on a continual basis with Core

Team phase review information, pipeline loading profile data, and strategic direction adjustments.

- The *pipeline loading profile* is used to monitor and maintain pipeline balance to maximize product development output. During strategic balancing, this profile is used to create an aggregate project schedule that is in balance with the company's development-related resource and skill capacity. On an ongoing basis, the profile is used to monitor the aggregate and functional pipelines. The aggregate pipeline loading profile is used as a "hard ceiling" to make sure that project and functional demands do not exceed the organization's resource capacity. The functional pipeline loading profiles, which are monitored for critical functional areas, are periodically reviewed to make sure that the functions and skills remain in balance, thus avoiding bottlenecks that would slow the entire pipeline.

- *Synchronized functional budgets* are arrived at differently than traditional functional budgets. Rather than looking at projects and functions independently, the strategic balancing process uses project needs and functional needs (maintenance, enhancements, capital equipment, process enhancements) as input and reconciles them with resource and capital constraints. Instead of projects and functions competing for scarce resources, they are motivated to work together to strategically maximize the output from these resources. These synchronized budgets must be flexible enough so that resources can be smoothly shifted across functional boundaries to resolve unforeseen project glitches.

All companies appear to have a semblance of strategic balancing through their annual planning and budgeting cycle; however, significant deficiencies exist that prevent senior management from providing true leadership for the pipeline. Typically, budgets are set by each function, independent of other functions except for overall reconciliation of the bottom line. Additionally, functional budgets frequently do not tie cleanly to the aggregate budgets of the cross-functional development projects. The result is that project leaders and functional managers are often pitted against each other because they are all trying to optimize performance for their area or team, frequently to the detriment of overall company performance.

A pipeline loading profile graphically shows the demand (projects requiring resources) and supply (resources available to work on projects) relationships *across* the various functional areas supporting product development over the long term. In most companies, the development-related resources are far out of balance across the functional areas because the focus on building staff for product development is usually on highly visible dedicated groups (typically R&D), while support groups (such as product management, manufacturing, and purchasing) are overlooked. A statement by the general manager at a major telecommunications equipment company illustrates this fallacy: "If I can hire another person, of course it will be a design engineer because I want more new products!" This same division had cut back overhead, decimating the purchasing group. Since purchasing could no longer adequately support product development, the design engineers were forced to take time from development to select vendors. The design engineers were extremely inefficient at working with vendors and their inexperience resulted in rampant material cost, delivery, and quality problems that threw the organization into crisis. Without the correct staffing ratios between functional areas involved in product development, pipeline performance is limited by the most overloaded function.

In areas of strategic importance where resource gaps exist, bold, long-term, functional plans can be put in place to build the organization, or a proactive search can begin to identify and qualify suitable partners or subcontractors (described later in more detail). This is very different from the standard budgetary approach, based on incremental changes from the prior year, that reinforces the status quo and delays needed organizational shifts until full-blown restructuring is necessary.

Pipeline Loading

While phase reviews are in place in many companies, they are not always used to optimize the development pipeline because each project is individually reviewed without consideration of other projects. The following example illustrates this common shortcoming. During the course of the phase review for Project X, questions arose about the ability to staff the project for success across all necessary functions. The marketing group was continually buried, handling urgent requests from the field and launching other products. Purchasing was overloaded, handling vendor delivery problems and working to reduce purchase price variance. A few key R&D team members were always on call to support problems in the field and the manufacturing line for existing products.

After a long discussion, the management team decided that the project was too important and had to move forward and the correct staff would be "found." Other concerns surfaced about the timing of this project and its ripple effect on other projects moving through development, but since the phase review was focused on one particular project, these concerns were assigned to a few senior managers to "investigate" off-line. At the conclusion of the phase review the project was given an enthusiastic approval by the senior management team. Subsequently the needed resources never appeared, overlap with other projects caused delays in bottleneck areas, and despite heroic efforts by the Core Team, the project got into trouble. Senior management was forced to pull resources from other projects to try to solve Project X's problems, causing additional pipeline chaos.

The underlying problem illustrated in this case was that the difficult decisions were not made at the original phase review because necessary cross-project information was not available to the PAC. In the absence of this information, the PAC used a zero-based budget mentality — "if the project makes sense then we've got to do it" — instead of recognizing its organization's true constraints and optimizing the deployment of its scarce resources. Even though phase reviews lead to better planning of *individual* projects, without effective pipeline loading, the overall pipeline can remain overloaded and thus sub-optimized.

These principles are well understood in the manufacturing environment, where starting a job without sufficiently available capacity leads to excess work-in-process inventory and low productivity. However, when a factory manager releases a work order, the capacity data and master build schedule are in front of him; this information is rarely available to the PAC faced with a decision to approve a project at a phase review.

With the necessary cross-project information, phase reviews are enhanced so that the PAC can optimize the overall pipeline. Strategic balancing, described in the previous section, through the aggregate project schedule shows how a particular project relates to the other development projects. Pipeline loading fine-tunes the aggregate project schedule to actively manage the entry and exit of development projects into the pipeline and seamlessly handle midcourse corrections. Capacity data is provided by the functional heads who make up the PAC so that the project can truly be staffed for success across all functions. Ultimately, pipeline loading drives an organization to focus on fewer, higher-impact projects that get to market much faster because resource shortfalls are avoided. In the words of the president of a medical instrument company that instituted pipeline loading, "I traded in eighty turtles for thirty-five racehorses."

Pipeline loading allocates effective development capacity between hard and soft commitments. Effective development capacity is based on the real level of resources available in each functional area after adjusting for administration, training, recruiting, turnover, vacation, and so on (often overlooked, these activities can represent a large portion of available time). Hard commitments include projects in the latter phases of development (after specification and planning are complete) and product support activities that require immediate resolution (which are often grossly underestimated). Soft commitments are those development activities that can be delayed or re-scoped. Obviously, if hard commitments alone exceed effective development capacity, then the pipeline simply will not be able to deliver. This is the situation that most companies face.

Managing the ratio of hard versus soft resource commitments within pipeline capacity is at the heart of pipeline optimization. The three factors governing this ratio are technology stability, launch flexibility, and project management performance.

- The less stable a technology is when it enters product development, the lower the hard commitment level must be, because when inevitable problems occur, resources will have to be pulled from soft commitments.

For example, low-end disk drive manufacturers are typically working with stable, proven technologies and can load their pipelines more heavily, whereas high-end disk drive manufacturers work with less stable, cutting-edge technologies and load their pipelines less heavily.

- Launch flexibility is based on how "locked-in" project schedules are, because if the end date cannot slip, then soft commitments must rise so that glitches in key development projects will not cause disaster. For example, automotive parts suppliers must contractually agree at the initiation of a project to deliver new parts on a specific date because the entire car platform schedule hinges on hundreds of suppliers delivering precisely on schedule. Consumer electronics manufacturers must release new products at scheduled industry trade shows that occur once or twice a year.
- Project management performance (Core Teams, phase reviews, structured methodology) contributes heavily to the predictability of project schedules and resource requirements. The better a company's project management performance, the more hard commitments can be made be cause fewer surprises in development will occur.

Figure 9–2 contrasts the pipeline loading of two companies. Company A uses pipeline loading to manage its pipeline. Company B does not have the information necessary to make the tough decisions between projects and thus has overcommitted. Company A has optimally utilized its resources in the prior and current periods and has a manageable balance between hard and soft commitments in future periods, which provides the basis for making resource allocation decisions on projects at upcoming phase reviews. Planned hard commitments are always below the effective capacity line so that all critical projects can be completed on an aggressive schedule. Soft commitments (for example, projects now in the concept phase that represent significant future resource commitments) are well over effective capacity but, since they can be delayed or re-scoped, provide the PAC with the flexibility to keep the pipeline running smoothly while keeping productivity high. This company consistently launches more products than its competition with shorter time-to-market because its resources are optimally deployed.

In contrast, company B has hard commitments that chronically exceed total capacity — which is far above effective capacity. The tendency in this company is to overload development in the mistaken belief that having more projects going will result in more products coming to market. Few commitments are soft because the company has fully committed to all the projects under development, typified by the CEO's (chief executive officer's) statement, "We don't kill projects here, we just wound them." Time-to-market is lengthy due to numerous delays caused by staffing shortfalls. Fire fighting is rampant, leading to low R&D productivity; thus fewer products are launched than expected. Dramatic improvements (as shown by the rising productivity line) are continually promised yet never achieved.

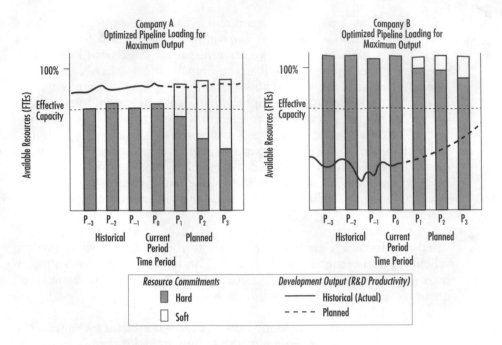

FIGURE 9–2   Aggregate pipeline profiles for two companies.

Aligning Functional Delivery

Functional managers are responsible for the flow of projects through their areas, and thus are actually managing a section of the development pipeline. The purpose of aligning functional delivery is to continually optimize the pipeline to achieve the maximum possible throughput. In this environment, functions and projects are integrated, not distinctly separate. Functional managers work together to improve the flow of projects through their collective functions. They no longer focus exclusively on their areas, but actively work with upstream and downstream functions to resolve problems rapidly.

Aligning functional delivery considers all activities that require resources across all development-related functions, including product development, technology development, and product support activities that are often underestimated (for example, marketing support, manufacturing troubleshooting, and sustaining engineering). Additionally, broad initiatives like implementing new systems and improving the development process must be taken into account. Of the above list, only product development activities are covered by Core Teams and phase reviews; the remaining activities are solely the responsibility of functional managers to deliver within the context of strategic balancing.

How a functional manager balances product development demands with functional objectives is governed by where the function falls on the spectrum from dedicated to shared, as shown in Figure 9–3. At one extreme, dedicated functions are focused exclusively on projects, such as a design group focused on a next-generation circuit design. Shared groups that are inundated with requests from many areas are at the other extreme. An example of this is a manufacturing reengineering group trying to support multiple development teams, troubleshoot on the factory floor, work with vendors, and so on. For dedicated groups, the challenge is to staff a project correctly or recommend that the project be delayed, re-scoped, or canceled. For shared groups, the challenge is to determine how to get out of the "victim mode" by creating an effective early warning system so that potential overloads can be identified and bottlenecks avoided.

Functional managers must be aware of what their groups are truly capable of delivering, and then work to keep commitments within these bounds through strategic balancing and pipeline loading. During strategic balancing, the functional managers must ensure that product strategy objectives are tightly interlocked with the effective development capacity in their functions (this "closing the loop" rarely occurs; thus most strategies remain unrealistic). During phase reviews at which the pipeline is loaded, all members of the PAC must guarantee that their functional areas can deliver on commitments. In our experience, most companies approve projects without sufficient resources in many areas, particularly shared functions, because effective development capacity is not understood.

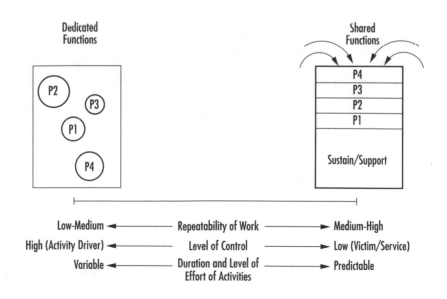

FIGURE 9–3   Spectrum of shared and dedicated functions.

Staffing projects is often difficult because each Core Team typically desires the best resources and usually more resources than are truly necessary. It falls to functional managers, working with Core Team members from various projects, to allocate their limited resources while still achieving functional objectives. By working closely with their respective Core Team members, functional managers can ensure that each project's plans are efficient and achievable. This exercise is simplified if quantified experience like cycle times from previous projects can be used as a starting point for fact-based planning.

Meanwhile functional managers must also staff their non-product development activities. Some of these activities, such as product support, are mandatory. The remaining activities should be focused on building the long-term capabilities of the function to handle the projects coming down the pipeline.

Simply having people work harder and longer to expand capacity is only a short-term solution, appropriate for temporary surges in workload. For functions to consistently deliver on longer-term plans, functional managers must shift from being reactive to anticipating requirements and proactively addressing limitations in the following ways:

- Ensuring staff flexibility by identifying other functional areas that have transferable skills that could be borrowed; cross-training individuals within the function to handle multiple jobs; beginning hiring cycles with sufficient lead time for recruiting, hiring, and training; and modifying the organization to leverage experience so that temporaries can be brought on board
- Reducing the development effort needed for a project by fostering re-use of proven designs and coordinating dialogue between projects to make the function's collective expertise available to each project
- Improving efficiency through streamlining the development process in the function, installing more sophisticated design tools, and upgrading the staff's skills
- Planning for outsourcing non-core competencies with sufficient lead time to identify, screen, and certify the contractors/alliance partners
- Ensuring that technologies are "on the shelf" when they are needed for future development projects by driving advanced development efforts and/or securing technology externally by building relationships — preferably exclusive — with cutting-edge vendors

In many companies that have improved their development process, functional managers find themselves with a diminished role of "supporting their Core Team members." In actuality, today's competitive environment increasingly demands a quantum leap in functional management performance. The key is to define the functional manager's role in terms of its essential contribution to pipeline management.

Supporting Systems

Optimizing a company's development pipeline should focus on management, not installing a sophisticated, computer-based resource scheduling system. For example, an advanced materials company had an information system designed and installed so that it had a detailed skills profile on every person, including staffing on projects projected for the next year. With this system, the company felt it would be able to instantly determine the optimal staff for any project and thus optimize its pipeline. In reality the system was rarely used and eventually shelved. The company found that it couldn't allocate people solely on their skill profile because this ignored many other intangible factors (such as attitude, energy level, and motivation). The system's complexity was so daunting that no one had the time to use it. There was no cross-functional forum of managers to do trade-offs and compromises. The company learned a costly lesson — that a data-handling tool can only *enable* pipeline management, not supplant it.

However, pipeline management can be very complex, due to the number of projects and sheer volume of data that must be analyzed and interpreted. Information technology can help in making strategic balancing, pipeline loading, and functional delivery work better. Decision-assistance tools help analyze data at a high level and systematically perform trade-offs without losing sight of priorities or getting bogged down. Data-handling tools are necessary to deal with the vast amount of information needed to analyze project priorities, understand resource and skill set loads, and perform pipeline analysis. Finally, these tools must be integrated with a company's business systems to avoid a high administrative burden.

Why Companies Have Problems Managing Their Product Development Pipeline

While most companies recognize that they don't effectively manage their product development pipeline, they fail to understand specifically what they are doing wrong. We see problems such as the following:

- They don't set priorities among the numerous opportunities and adjust the organization's capabilities to deliver new products.
- The entry and exit of development projects into the pipeline isn't actively managed.
- Product development isn't aligned with functional management.
- They expect a system to magically manage the problem.

References

1. Our earlier work on pipeline management can be found in the *Product Development and Management Association's Handbook on Product Development* (New York: John Wiley & Sons, 1996).

2. Michael E. McGrath, *Strategic Balance, Product Strategy for High-Technology Companies* (Burr Ridge, Ill.: Irwin Professional Publishing, 1995), 232–258.

3. For a discussion of aggregate project planning, see Steven C. Wheelwright and Kim B. Clark, *Revolutionizing Product Development* (New York: The Free Press, 1992), 86–110.

CHAPTER 10

Stages in the Evolution of the Product Development Process

Amram R. Shapiro

Every company that really improves the new product development process goes through evolutionary stages. Some do it faster than others and with fewer detours, but fast or slow, every company that gets to world class must evolve through these stages to get there. There are no shortcuts.

This evolution is to be expected for a complex system or process such as new product development. In a system, only certain combinations of elements work together coherently Taken together, these are the characteristic process elements of a stage. In a sense new product development is only as strong as its weakest link. Adding an element from a later stage prematurely is usually pointless, just as adding a turbocharger to a bicycle won't make it go faster — it just adds weight.

Different performance standards are expected at each stage. This is one of the strongest findings in our benchmark studies of product development best practices and performance. As companies advance through the stages, performance improves, usually in a step function. Development cycle time is highly sensitive to development stage. So are measures such as wasted development or R&D effectiveness. Predictability of results gets better too. And within each stage there is an opportunity for continuous improvement, as the practices of that stage become second nature to the organization.

In this chapter we will describe each of these stages, along with their typical elements and standards of performance. Understanding each stage enables a company to position itself and determine what improvements should be made next. This provides earlier recognition of the opportunities for improvement and a realistic assessment of the effort required to make the next step change.

Evolving toward Product And Cycle-time Excellence

There are four stages in the evolution of new product development (see Figure 10–1).

- *Stage 0* — Necessary elements of a product development process are either missing or extremely weak. The approach is informal and ad hoc and the failure of product development threatens the survival of the business or company.
- *Stage 1* — This is the classic stage during which project management responsibilities are distributed across functional organizations, and coordination is often difficult and time-consuming.
- *Stage 2* — This stage is characterized by the cross-functional integration of project management at many levels, from the Core Team to the Product Approval Committee. The result is short cycle times and little wasted development. The principal challenge to master in this stage is implementing effective cross-functional project management structures and skills.
- *Stage 3* — This stage integrates planning at the enterprise or cross-project level with the excellent execution achieved in Stage 2. Product strategy and technology planning are linked to the project management. The entire product development pipeline is managed to optimize strategic benefit. The principal challenge to master in this stage is implementation of cross-project management processes.

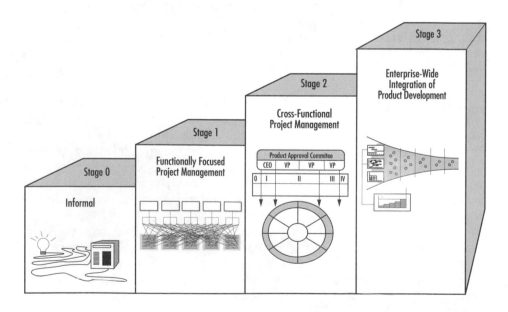

FIGURE 10–1   Typical stages in the evolution of Product And Cycle-time Excellence.

Companies must progress through stages because of constraints on rates of organizational change. Companies can only absorb so much change at a time, typically less than the many reengineering or other improvement efforts they undertake. It takes time to properly implement the elements of a stage in the evolution of new product development. It also takes time for them to become second nature to an organization. (A good rule of thumb is that it takes one to two years to fully master a stage.) That is why it's critical to understand the next elements that are essential to advancement, so that the focus can be put on these while other best practices are deferred until later.

In practice, many companies try to do too much. How many corporations, for example, suffer from initiative overload? Where management has championed many new programs simultaneously (Malcolm Baldrige, ISO-9000, JIT, quality circles, QFD, customer focus, innovation, employee involvement, management by objectives, shareholder value creation, and so on), the organization often cannot absorb them all. Employees learn to pay them lip service and wait for the next "program of the month." Management can only implement a very few initiatives at one time.

Corporations are bounded by one simple constraint: they can be truly superior in only a few attributes. Some companies are marked by functional excellence, others by excellence in a critical business process. Excellence is built and maintained through consistency and focus, and the particular strengths of a given company are those embedded in its culture, organization, and operations. These strengths are usually the ones that originally built the company and are most highly prized. This kind of consistency can be maintained for only a few key strengths.

Companies that are truly superior in one area or another tend to worry about maintaining that superiority. 3M, for example, is noted not only for its record of innovation, but also for the amount of time and attention it spends on self-assessment and keeping track of its innovation record. Not satisfied with being used so often in the business press as an example of good innovation practices, 3M periodically reviews those practices to check whether it is living up to its press, and the company maintains an extraordinary database of project data that help it to understand which factors are predictors of project success. Companies such as DuPont, Motorola, and IBM regularly assess their stage of advancement. Motorola does annual quality audits. DuPont uses a variant of this framework to perform what it calls Continuous Improvement Assessments.

The implication of so much cultural inertia is that moving from one stage to the next is very difficult. However, it's probably just as difficult for a company's competitors, and reaching a higher stage may create a competitive advantage. This achievement is likely to be sustainable, because the change is just as hard to reverse as it was to make in the first place.

A summary of the main characteristics of each stage in the evolution toward Product And Cycle-time Excellence is shown in Table 10–1, and will be described in the following sections.

TABLE 10-1   Characteristics in the stages of evolution toward Product And Cycle-time Excellence.

	Stage 0	Stage 1	Stage 2	Stage 3
Product Development Process (Structure and Definition)	None Concern about just getting the product out overwhelms any consideration of process Weak project management discipline	Distinct functional processes Hard to coordinate Adherence to process varies widely	The process is structured and clearly but simply defined A single overall process integrates all functions Used on all projects	Process is ingrained in the culture Product development process is formally linked to product strategy and technology processes
Project Team Organization	Ad hoc Firefighters often more highly regarded than project managers	Inconsistent team membership Functional politics strong Leadership shifts or is indeterminate	Small dedicated cross-functional teams similar to Core Team model Strong project management	Experienced Core Teams often develop multiple generations of products Core Teams are used for platform and technology development
Management Decision Process	Informal and highly reactive Resources flow to whatever catches management's attention	Priorities are set through annual budgeting Project status reporting is initiated but is time consuming Functional managers set de facto, often conflicting, priorities Resource allocation is very difficult	Efficient, event-based Phase Review process is used by a decisive cross-functional management team (e.g., PAC) to set priorities Priorities are accompanied by resources	Decisions are based on fully developed product and technology strategies Priorities set within context of overall pipeline and skill mix plans Product platform decisions get an increased focus of attention
Continuous Improvement	Individual learning takes place, but is not captured in a process	Process elements are owned by individual functions; key skills often known only to certain individuals It's hard to learn from failed projects because of fear of being blamed	Full-time process owner in place Process is evaluated regularly and updated Opportunities to advance to next stage identified	Process is "owned" by all who use it There is a history of process upgrades and extensions Opportunities to advance the state of the art regularly identified
Target Setting/Metrics	No process targets Focus is often on survival or financial turnaround	Overall process targets not set or set by management fiat Current performance is hard to measure	Process targets are routinely set and measured against These include cycle time and quality measures	Process targets are set based on quantitative benchmarking of world-class companies Annual improvements of 5%–15% in all major metrics routinely planned

Product Strategy Process	No process in place, only the de facto implications of past decisions. Tendency to follow inconsistent strategies	Strategic visions inconsistent and not linked with product strategy. Tendency to attempt too much or be all things to all customers	Focus is on individual products, not platforms. Product strategy is done in annual planning, if at all. Product strategy issues raised in phase reviews tend to be dealt with informally	Focus is on product platforms, current and new. Product strategy is a formal process. It is linked to technology planning and executed through efficient product development process
Technology Management Process	No distinction between technology and product development	This is a functional responsibility. Finger pointing between marketing and technical functions is common. Large resource swings year to year are common	Typically no formal process for technology planning. Distinction between technology and product development becomes clearer, but not managed	Technology strategy is linked to product strategy. Technology development is more deliberately managed. Technology transfer to product development process is well defined
Pipeline Management	Pipeline not managed or balanced. Fire fighting gets disproportionate share of resources	Project proliferation is common. Chronic bottlenecks occur in certain functions	Distribution of projects by phase is known. Fewer projects staffed. Skill mix problems still common	The strategic distribution of projects is known and managed. Skill mix management is long term
Time to Market Performance	Not measured or managed. May be infinite	Inconsistent and unpredictable. Very hard to measure. Tendency to bring many products to market before they are fully debugged, so manufacturing problems or high levels of engineering changes are common	40%–60% of Stage 1. Cycle times are based on completing development of a quality product which is manufacturable in volume and at acceptable yields	Best in industry and declining. Combined with product strategy advantages which focus effort on right products, the advantage is very hard for competitors to overcome
Development Productivity	Not measured or managed. Typically very low	Many projects are canceled late or never brought to market. Slow time to market limits productivity. Revenues from new products lag industry leaders	Reduced time to market greatly increases productivity. Greatly reduced wasted R&D since phase reviews lead to earlier cancellation. Revenues from new products increasing	Little wasted R&D. All efforts highly focused by platform, technology, and product. High percentage of sales generated by new products and new platforms

Stage 0

Companies in Stage 0 have neither a structured development process in place nor mature enough functional or project management skills to overcome this lack of structure. This is the informal stage, when every development project is done as if it were the first. There is no consistent model for project organization. Ad hoc teams are formed and changed as the organization reacts to external pressures. In this reactive environment, resources flow to the projects that catch management's attention. Often these are fire-fighting efforts designed to fix problems or satisfy an unhappy customer. Without a process in place to improve and measure, the only learning is individual, and the only performance measurement is the overall financial condition of the company. Advanced processes such as product strategy, technology management, and pipeline management are not even thought about as processes.

Companies in Stage 0 have difficulty bringing a regular flow of successful products to market. The occasional success cannot always be followed by supporting product introductions, making competitive gains hard to sustain. Development cycle times are totally unpredictable for an individual project, but overall are very long, with a large percentage of projects never making it to completion. Pipeline metrics are not kept, but if they were, they would show a high percentage of development resources devoted to non-development activities, such as technical service or manufacturing support.

Most viable companies have evolved to Stage 1 and beyond, but a surprising number are either in Stage 0 or have some of the characteristics of Stage 0 companies. Some Stage 0 companies have one strong function (e.g., engineering) and several weak ones (e.g., manufacturing or marketing). For example, a biotechnology firm built around the credentials of its academic founders might have to turn to an established pharmaceutical firm to take its product to market. Some Stage 1 companies may neglect their development practices, and the structure that was in place implodes. As a result they regress to Stage 0.

The main challenge for Stage 0 companies is to address their functional weaknesses while developing some of the discipline that new product development demands, such as basic project management skills. If a Stage 0 company addresses its product development and project management weaknesses *functionally*, it advances to Stage 1. If it is ready to put in the additional effort to improve the product development process *cross-functionally*, it may advance directly to Stage 2, but the effort and commitment required should not be minimized.

Stage 1

The theme of Stage 1 is functional mastery. The problems of Stage 0 resulting from specific functional weaknesses and imbalances have been overcome as each function develops its own competencies and practices. Unlike Stage 0, with its informal and ad hoc processes, in Stage 1 there are documented and repeatable processes developed and applied at the functional level. The organizational structure is also functional. With so much emphasis on functional excellence, much of the energy of companies entrenched in Stage 1 is devoted to finding ways to link functions.

Product development is seen as a functional responsibility. In some companies, one function — engineering or R&D or marketing — is seen as having overall responsibility for product development. In others, lead responsibility shifts from function to function at various points in the product development process. These transfer points are often points of great conflict and difficulty. They become interfunctional battlefields, especially when "throwing development over the wall" to the next function includes transferring responsibility for problems that may not have been fixed earlier in the development process. "Over-the-wall" transfers are common in Stage 1 because there are so many walls.

Companies try many ways to improve these hand-offs. Sometimes they create very detailed process documentation to capture every functional responsibility and cross-function dependency. These tend to be overly complex and inflexible and fall into disuse. More effort seems to be devoted to carefully defining the mutual responsibilities of the functions than to finding ways to streamline their interactions.

Sometimes Stage 1 companies try to improve their serial process by finding ways to move the walls. For example, some companies ask manufacturing engineers to take on some of the development engineers' responsibilities as a way of ensuring that these activities are completed before ramp-up. In one organization the documentation group found itself creating the product functional specifications, which were only loosely produced during the development process and never frozen.

In Stage 1, project organization is better than in Stage 0, but still lacks dedicated and consistent team membership and an appropriate role for project managers. Team membership is inconsistent project to project and tends to change as the project advances through the functional maze. Functional managers don't hesitate to change team membership if their priorities shift.

Stage 1 companies tend to have relatively weak project managers. Their role is more one of administrators, record keepers, or facilitators than leaders. We sometimes call such project managers "I, Claudius" project managers; they would keep the records while Rome burned. They record the history of the project but don't powerfully influence its course.

Schedule accuracy is notoriously poor in this stage, with slippages made evident to management as late as possible. Because responsibility for the project tends to shift, the schedules often cover only portions of the development project. Those making these functional schedules may not feel ownership of the overall schedule set at the project outset. As a result, overall schedules tend to lack integrity and are not regularly updated or reconciled. Performance to schedule may not be reported to management on a timely basis since nobody has this overall responsibility. When we ask developers in Stage 1 organizations to show us their project schedules, the common answer is, "Which one do you want to see?"

Because authority and responsibility tend to reside more in the functions than in the development project team, accountability is often unclear. When we look at troubled development projects in Stage 1 companies, there is a pattern of shifting responsibilities through the life of the project. Decisions made by one function are undone by another. Each hand-off is an opportunity to redefine the project. The greater allegiance of development team members to their functions than to the overall business or project leads them to parochial decisions. When things go wrong, the functions tend to blame each other, often in sharp memos full of statements such as "Marketing believes . . . ,"or "Engineering thinks . . . ," or "Manufacturing feels . . ."

The management decision making in Stage 1 organizations often evolves to one based on sign-off procedures. This is a time-consuming and politically charged activity. The sign-off decision can be pocket-vetoed by any of the critical functions, and there is no urgency built into the procedure. When problems arise, for example over differing visions of what a product should be, a sign-off process can grind development to a halt. In disciplined organizations, this results in delay. In more free-form organizations, it leads to deferred resolution of the open issue. Developers go forward without all the signatures required and hope for the best. If problems arise, those who withheld their signatures tend to disavow the project.

Budgeting is the mechanism used to set priorities. Annual allocations are made to individual functions, which are then expected to allocate their resources to individual development projects. Conflicting priorities are common, sub-optimizing the allocation of resources to the overall business and causing delay.

In the absence of decisive phase reviews, management tends to require frequent status reporting from development teams, a time-consuming and largely ineffective mechanism for providing senior management oversight of projects.

Continuous improvement in Stage 1 is done at the level of functional processes. Given the focus in Stage 1 on functional excellence, it is not unusual to find that certain functional steps have been well defined and documented, but it is also not unusual to find other equally important steps not defined or documented at all. For example, a world-class test operation may operate in an otherwise inefficient development process. Superior estimating rules of thumb may have been developed in an environment that regularly produces cost overruns. No one improves the cross-functional linkages. No one can really "own" and improve the overall process since the separate functional elements are too jealously guarded. There is little incentive for parallelism or concurrent engineering. The downstream functions, such as manufacturing and service, tend not to get involved in a project until quite late. Because it is so difficult and costly to make changes in a development project in later stages, this absence of parallelism produces both cost overruns and time delays.

Stage 1 companies may collect good metrics within a function but rarely have good overall process metrics. Without good development metrics, such as time-to-market or wasted development, it is hard to set sound targets for improvement. It is also hard to set accurate targets for individual projects, and not surprisingly, forecast accuracy in Stage 1 tends to be poorer than in later stages, when cycle-time guidelines provide a sound baseline for target setting.

In the absence of objective performance targets, senior managers tend to dictate their own. They may cut proposed schedules in half in the belief that they are padded, or impose a release date because of a perceived market window. Developers tend to ignore or become demoralized by such imposed targets. Some developers even keep two schedules, one that they show to management and the real one that they use to guide project activities. All this leads to lack of correlation between targets established at the outset of projects and actual performance.

Product strategy tends to be undisciplined in Stage 1. If long-range product planning is done, it is in the marketing function and may not be linked to the actual programs being launched. It is common to attempt to do too much, or to be all things to all customers. With development cycle times longer than internally admitted, the horizon of product planning tends to be too short. The focus is on the next product, not the product as part of a product line, or the product line as part of a product platform. This leads to an opportunistic, non-strategic selection process.

A similar problem occurs in basic technology development. The fundamental separation of the functions leads to decisions to invest in technology that are not necessarily linked to business or strategic objectives. R&D managers work to maintain independence in selecting what programs to support, because they do not trust the marketing functions to think long-term or in visionary ways. There are generally too many projects and periodic (and mostly ineffective) purges of programs as attempts are made to get a better balance between programs and resources.

Stage 1 companies can reliably get new products to market, but their cycle times are quite long, about twice that of Stage 2 companies. Inefficient management decision making leads to late cancellations of projects, and much higher percentages of wasted development than in Stage 2. Pressures to get products to market prematurely often lead to high costs in the late stages or even after product introduction.

The Stage 1 levels of performance are still barely competitive in some industries, which have been late to improve their product development practices, but won't continue to be for long. In highly time-compressed industries such as electronics, this is no longer a viable stage.

The main challenge for Stage 1 companies is to achieve cross-functional integration of product development at the project level and all the benefits that come with this step improvement.

Stage 2

In Stage 2, companies make a tremendous advance. By integrating all of the functions involved in the execution of product development projects, they dramatically decrease cycle time and increase development efficiency.

A single overall process integrates all of the functions. It is clearly defined and simply structured. It incorporates the best of the functional subprocesses developed in Stage 1, streamlined and incorporating the optimal level of concurrence and overlap. In mature Stage 2 companies, the process coverage is complete: 100% of appropriate projects use the process.

In Stage 2, small, dedicated cross-functional teams such as Core Teams are the norm. Membership is standardized, often with variants for more or less complex or sizable projects. These teams effectively represent their functions in all matters of project execution. As a team, they take responsibility for their projects, thereby reducing the interfunctional bickering so common in Stage 1. They are led by project leaders who are very effective at working through their cross-functional teams to achieve project objectives.

Management decision making is enormously improved in Stage 2. A decisive cross-functional management team, such as the Product Approval Committee (PAC), is in place. An efficient, event-based Phase Review Process brings the development teams before management at key decision points. The frequent status reporting of Stage 1 is abandoned as time-consuming and inconclusive. Every phase review leads to a decision, so that the decision-making delays that our analysis has shown contribute up to 40% of all wasted development are eliminated.

Because these integrated management teams include both those with responsibility for setting the strategic course of the business and those who control the major resource pools, there is much less likelihood of decision making at cross purposes. A decision to go with the project is also a decision to commit resources to it. This cross-functional integration at both the senior management and Core Team level leads to great consistency in decision making.

Whereas scheduling was largely arbitrary in Stage 1, in Stage 2 scheduling is based on cycle-time guidelines. These guidelines are developed for each step of the process and may vary with the characteristics of projects, such as complexity and the degree of reliance on new technology. These step guidelines are periodically revised as the process improves. Cycle-time guidelines are in effect standard costing for time. They improve setting a project schedule by focusing on the content of development, not on evaluations of the motives of those preparing the schedules. With increased schedule accuracy, a company in Stage 2 more rationally schedules projects and allocates resources, leading to fewer underfunded projects.

Stage 2 organizations make use of concurrent engineering. Because of the involvement of all the major functions from beginning to end of the project, there are strong incentives to do the job correctly from the beginning. Manufacturing has input in the early stages, and developers do not abandon the project when it is time to scale it up. The use of dedicated teams and structured development produces a high degree of parallelism and overlap between development activities.

The role of the functions in Stage 2 development is as critical as ever, but it is clearly distinguished from the responsibility for developing individual products. Functions now have the principal responsibility of maintaining and deepening their skills and providing the necessary resources for individual development projects. (This is the beginning of the skill mix aspect of pipeline management, the process that will be perfected in Stage 3.)

For the first time, in Stage 2, companies are able to set really meaningful targets for new product development process performance. In Stage 1, historical baselines of performances are hard to find and predictions of future performance are very inaccurate or overly cautious. In Stage 2, by contrast, there are historical baselines and entitlements based on what the process can do. Full-time process owners, sometimes called PACE engineers or PACE managers, are in place and regularly upgrade the process and set new process targets. One of the key responsibilities of the process owner is to identify the opportunity to advance to the next stage.

Companies in Stage 2 currently find themselves in the top 20% in terms of time-to-market and product quality. The time-to-market in Stage 2 is typically 40%–60% of that in Stage 1. Clearly, the move from Stage 1 to Stage 2 is one of the greatest improvements that a company can make. This is the stage a company must be at to be competitive. Any company that cannot meet the performance standards of Stage 2 will be at the mercy of companies that can.

Individual phase reviews tend to raise issues that Stage 2 companies have not yet developed mature processes to address. These are the cross-project issues of product strategy, technology management, and pipeline management. To some extent, all are dealt with in de facto ways in Stage 2. In Stage 3, establishing *processes* for each is the main challenge.

Stage 3

Once companies have achieved cross-functional integration at the project level, they are in a position to achieve the next quantum step: cross-functional integration at the enterprise level. This is Stage 3, enterprise-wide integration of product development. In this stage companies add the cross-project elements of PACE, those elements that help companies to align their product development with their long-term strategic vision and optimize their development portfolios.

Several new processes are added in this stage and integrated with those of Stage 2. Notably, these are the product strategy process and the technology planning process. Pipeline management, which begins in Stage 2, is now brought to a greater level of sophistication. Finally, the project management elements of PACE, installed in Stage 2, are further refined and streamlined in Stage 3. As the practices of Stage 2 become widely shared and understood, they require less formal description or policing.

In Stage 3, reliance on dedicated cross-functional teams such as Core Teams is now fully established. These development teams tend to be highly experienced. It's not unusual in Stage 3 companies for the same team to develop succeeding generations of the same product. The value of this long-term dedication is enormous. It produces learning-curve improvements and facilitates easy communication among team members.

World-class companies compare themselves to other world-class competitors as reference points for target setting. Targets are often stretch goals that other companies would consider impossible to achieve. These same goals, if set in earlier stages, would be unrealistic and counterproductive. The assumption is that new product development can continually improve, and efforts are always underway to achieve those improvements. More often than not, these Stage 3 companies provide the benchmarks to which other competitors compare themselves.

One of the key indicators of Stage 3 status is that confidence in the product development process is so high that business strategies explicitly work to exploit this advantage. This exploitation may take several forms. In some cases, it will include attempts to overwhelm competitors through the rapid introduction of many new products. In other cases it takes the form of carefully timed new product launches to exploit trade shows or other events in the buying cycle. In industries with annual new product introduction cycles, for example, a development cycle shorter than twelve months offers enormous advantages. There is a built-in cushion for technical or competitive surprises. More time can be devoted up front on customer interactions to define product requirements. Increased reliability in terms of delivering on product announcements builds customer, distributor, and stock market confidence.

Stage 3 companies typically view the new product development process as a strategic advantage. This attitude naturally reinforces the time and effort they devote to maintaining this leading position. These companies have the best development cycle times in their industry and are usually gaining in market share as a result.

Using the Stages Model to Drive Advancement

The stages model of the evolution of product development has many uses. Used as an assessment tool, this framework can help a company to be clear-sighted in assessing its strengths and weaknesses. It can also be used as a continuous improvement tool to check on progress against targeted improvements. In large, multidivisional corporations, it can be used to compare business units or divisions. But the most important use of all is to help companies to set priorities for the implementation of improvements to their product development process. When used by an experienced implementor, it is a particularly powerful tool.

When using the stages model, it is important to remember that a company's overall standing is not a function of the strongest or weakest element, but is established by the overall pattern. Since each stage is the foundation on which the next is built, it is important to pay attention to the key challenges of the next stage. A Stage 0 company must improve its functional and basic project management skills to get benefit from other process improvements. A Stage 1 company must make its project management and execution truly cross-functional. A Stage 2 company must integrate the cross-project management elements with the project management to create a powerful enterprise-wide system. A Stage 3 company must take full strategic and competitive advantage of the superior performance of its development process.

Advancing from one stage to the next offers such tremendous advantages that it is worth the effort, but the effort should not be minimized. Each step change is a major undertaking, requiring significant commitment from senior managers and involving change at every level in the organization. Each step change takes time to implement properly and to embed in the routine and culture of a company. To move from Stage 1 to Stage 3 will take a company two to three years if it follows the stages "road map." Companies that try too much or too little at once, or don't actually develop implementation plans, take much longer and do not advance as far. Companies that advance steadily stage to stage will gain a sustainable and enduring advantage.

Summary

Product development evolves through well-defined stages at all companies, and understanding this evolution helps a company see where it is and where it wants to go.

- In Stage 0, product development is an informal process, and certain functional and project management skills are lacking.
- In Stage 1, product development responsibilities are distributed across strong functional organizations.
- In Stage 2, there is cross-functional integration at the project level. This is the first true step toward Product And Cycle-time Excellence.
- In Stage 3, the most successful product development organizations achieve cross-functional integration at the enterprise level.
- PACE is a process for moving from Stages 0 and 1 to Stages 2 and 3.

CHAPTER 11

Implementing PACE: How to Make It Real and Make It Lasting

Amram R. Shapiro
Dean P. Gilmore

Prior to this chapter we focused on the whys and whats of PACE — its benefits and its seven elements. Here we will discuss some insights into the hows of PACE — how to implement it and make it stick. Our experience, coupled with the knowledge gained from our ongoing benchmarking surveys, shows that many companies begin with the intention to implement a product development process similar to PACE, but don't achieve the benefits that others do. This performance gap can only be explained by differences in implementation. The most successful firms have recognized that there is a best-practice way to implement best practices.

Because changing the way an organization develops products affects all functions and all levels of management, this entails major cultural change. Such change is difficult because people have operated for years in the present culture and may have been successful to a certain degree. Now the rules of the game are changing and many will resist these changes, even though the future viability of the company may be at stake. Adjusting to cultural change is difficult because many of the rules are never made explicit. A company's culture is often largely invisible to those within it.

We have helped many companies implement PACE successfully and embed the changes within the culture and have encountered the impediments to success and overcome them. We have also studied how many companies have attempted to make fundamental improvements to product development only to find them ineffective or short-lived. The improvements never became truly institutionalized or ingrained in the culture. This is the goal of implementation: demonstrable, measurable, and widespread improvement that is self-sustaining and part of a new culture of continuous improvement.

The Implementation Experience: Mixed Reviews

A computer company we visited was typical of many companies. After years of phenomenal growth, it was facing a host of difficulties. Growth was slowing, at least in part because of protracted product development efforts. Products were announced but didn't ship. Although some competitors slipped too, others hit the market window in full stride and took significant market share. One of the delayed new products was introduced under pressure before the bugs had been ironed out. Service costs were extremely high as problems at the customer sites were addressed on the fly. There were so many changes to the design that the change order process was overwhelmed. Manufacturing ramp-up was delayed by all of this turmoil. Customers, many of them long-time loyalists, were complaining. One salesman confided to us that he was recommending that his customers not place orders; instead, he offered deep discounts on older-generation equipment. Within the organization, morale was at a low ebb. Engineers on the troubled projects were living at the company, putting in eighty hours or more a week. Two highly regarded engineers, one in hardware and one in software, had recently left to join a smaller competitor, and rumors that resumés were on the street were common. "I'll tell you one thing for sure," one weary project manager told us, "I'll never go through this again."

Recognizing that something needed to be done, the vice president of engineering organized an internal task force. The team reviewed the current process, which was highly informal. Postmortems, as they were called, were held for several recently completed projects, detailing many specific problems and much dissatisfaction. It was decided that a new process was needed. A small team was assigned the task. It worked diligently and after several months produced a document describing the new development process, which was issued to the whole organization. This was done with much fanfare, including the distribution of laminated cards showing a simplified high-level overview of the new process. Several project teams tried to use the process but for various reasons didn't follow through. Some were already too far along. Others encountered specific difficulties in following the document's recommendations. All found something to object to. One team felt it was too busy even to read it. The team that created the document met with many groups to encourage adoption. More often than not, these meetings turned into gripe sessions. Gradually the authors lost interest and moved into positions that would subject them to less abuse. Six months after publication, not a single project was using the new process. Some people still had their laminated cards and used the high-level stage names to describe their project status, but the 3-inch vinyl notebook detailing the process was sitting on shelves, unopened and unused.

Why Implementation Is Difficult

Why is it so difficult for organizations to change? Why do so many companies make sincere efforts to improve product development without true success? In our experience there are at least eight reasons why companies find this so difficult to achieve. Some of these relate to beliefs about what the change entails. Others relate to underestimation of the effort required, or belief in piecemeal approaches or quick fixes. Some relate to the approaches used to implement these changes. Together they provide a good summary of the impediments to successful implementation.

1. *Awareness.* An absolute prerequisite for change is a common understanding of the current conditions, why they must change, and how, specifically, they must change. Since product development cuts across many functional areas, each with different problems and viewpoints, rarely is a common understanding of the underlying problems obvious. Rather there is a general feeling that one must do better, coupled with sniping between functions. The realization that shared survival is at stake is buried.

Some companies have also investigated the best practices of companies that are leaders in product development. This can provide proof that better methods exist, with shorter cycle times and more effective team structures. Rarely, however, do companies know how to tailor and implement these practices in their own organization based solely on these studies.

2. *Development not viewed as an integrated process.* Another significant impediment is the lack of understanding that product development is a fundamental business process involving all members of all functions. Many companies have not yet realized that this is one of the most important business processes that they manage. Without this realization, they tend to focus their energies on improving the next development effort or on specific functional improvements but not the overall development process. Recognizing that improving the development process is one of the most valuable initiatives a manager can undertake is vital to the success of the implementation.

3. *Who owns the problem?* Product development is, by its nature, cross-functional and involves many management layers. If development times are slow, whose problem is it? In a sense, it is everyone's problem, but that observation is too broad to be helpful. In most organizations the problems of product development are seen as belonging to some function or another, and the temptation is to expect that function to fix it on its own. This may be R&D in some organizations, or engineering or marketing. In fact, it is highly unusual

The Keys to Successful PACE Implementation

We have found that there are four keys to successful PACE implementation; they are the ways to overcome the impediments we've just described. They overcome the inertia and skepticism in the organization. Every successful PACE implementation makes use of all of them.

1. *Getting ready.* An organization must be ready before it will change. Successful PACE implementations are preceded by activities that clarify and focus understanding of the need to improve the product development process for all functional areas and levels of management. Some companies are proactive and adopt a leading-edge process in anticipation of its benefits. Unfortunately, in many companies it takes a crisis such as a revenue decline, a major product failure, or the loss of key people before the organization comes to the realization of the magnitude of the changes required.

2. *Planning.* Since PACE is a complex process cutting across the entire organization, an explicit, detailed, and well-understood implementation plan is critical. The first step is to determine the goals, or targets, of the implementation. These targets include timing of the roll-out to all development programs, reduction in development cycle time, and increased development productivity and R&D effectiveness. These targets clearly identify what is at stake for the organization and the expected benefits.

The next step is to develop an implementation plan with the correct actions, sequence, and responsibilities. One dilemma is that the implementor can easily identify more areas that need fixing than can possibly be tackled at once. The implementor is a bit like a triage nurse who deals with the life-threatening problems first and postpones other areas until later. Obviously, this plan must be well thought out and based on experience, or the patient may die.

An equipment supplier to the cable TV industry completed an investigation into problems with its product development process. The division president, after hearing recommendations for improvement, latched onto the Core Team as the solution to his problems. Several of his vice presidents cautioned him that a plan was needed to carefully roll out all elements of PACE. After brushing aside their concerns, the president put a Core Team in charge of a group of important projects. Other, more important, problems with the development process were ignored. Soon the lone Core Team dissolved in frustration, with the organization becoming even more disillusioned than before.

3. *Building gradually.* In implementation it is crucial to build gradually and learn by doing. Organizations can only absorb so much change at once. To assist the change process, training in various forms must, of course, be provided to Core Teams, middle managers, and the PAC. However, we have found that traditional training practices, in which the entire organization is trained at once (for example, TQM [total quality management] training), are not effective when

implementing a major process improvement. Instead, training is more effective if done just in time, meaning training only those who will apply the new methods and immediately before they begin their work.

A consumer electronics company achieved substantial improvements in its early application of PACE concepts to a few projects. Delighted with the results, the president decided to roll out the process to all development projects concurrently. The result was chaos — teams weren't properly trained, cross-project management techniques were not yet in place, management was not capable of directing all the teams at once. Very quickly the initial gains in product development process improvements were lost.

4. *Continuous improvement.* Continuous improvement is the path to world-class performance. For continuous improvement to occur, everyone in the organization has to be involved and a specific group designated with its primary purpose to continue to improve the process and combat the tendency toward complacency.

A data communications company, after fully implementing an improved product development process, formed a PACE group headed by a director-level individual. This group facilitates development projects, conducts ongoing training, works with functional managers to improve cycle time in their areas, benchmarks other leading companies to learn new methods, and continues to identify additional opportunities for improvement. After the initial dramatic improvement, this company's product development cycle time continues to decrease 10%–15% per year.

Applying PACE to Multiple Industries

While there are many similarities in product development processes across companies, there are obviously differences as well. PACE, as a flexible, comprehensive tool kit of best practices for product development, has been extensively customized to fit the specific needs of different industries and companies. The following are just a few examples of client engagements, showing how industry characteristics are addressed during implementation.

1. *Semiconductor devices and process industries.* In semiconductor devices and process industries, process development is often at least as important and time-consuming as product, application, or device design. For semiconductors, for example, development of the fabrication process requires intensive effort and enormous capital expenditures. In the chemical industry, product and process must often be developed together. The main implication is that PACE in these industries stands for Product/Process And Cycle-time Excellence. Throughout a project both product and process development issues must be addressed.

2. *Complex system products.* Complex products with multiple electronic, software, and mechanical subassemblies frequently need to distinguish

12. *Multidivisional corporations.* One of the advantages of the breadth of PACE is that it can be applied across multiple divisions within a large corporation, even if those divisions are very different. A common product development process promotes cooperation across divisions, including joint development efforts, and makes it possible to integrate resources throughout the company. A common process does not mean the same process. The phases may have the same requirements (and link similarly to other processes, such as capital approval), but the specific steps may vary from division to division.

Leading the Change in the Product Development Process

Finally, successfully implementing a world-class product development process involves the efforts of many people. It doesn't just happen and won't happen if the right people are not actively involved in the implementation.

Management

Managers from all functions, senior individual contributors, technical specialists, and technical managers all play a significant role in changing the product development process. They have the prime responsibility to define and implement the details of the new process.

Their role begins with defining the changes necessary to the current product development process. This requires understanding the current process as well as the specific opportunities for improvement. The changes need to make sense as both part of an overall architecture and individually. This initially involves defining an overall decision-making process, such as a Phase Review Process, establishing an effective approach to project-team organization like the Core Team approach, and clearly structuring the detailed activities of product development. Following that, the other elements of the overall product development process — product strategy, technology management, design techniques and development tools, and cross-project management — need to be upgraded.

Managers also need to guide the implementation of the changes. This is particularly challenging because process changes such as this are cross-functional and involve the cooperative effort of those with different objectives. This requires managers from all functional areas to make compromises for the greater good of the company as a whole.

In our experience in implementing improvements to the product development process, this is where the best middle managers stand out. They rise above the others to lead the change, putting in the extra effort and making the personal sacrifices necessary. Changing a process as complex and involved as product development is not easy, and only the best will be able to do it.

Facilitation

We have been describing an implementation approach derived through practice and experience. It requires a clear vision of how successful implementation is achieved, wedded to a practical ability to make midcourse corrections and adjust the process.

Implementation of a broad and complex process like product development requires facilitation. It cannot be done simply by edict. As was mentioned previously, thousands of things need to change, and there is resistance and confusion when the change is actually required.

Implementation can succeed without an outside facilitator such as an implementation consultant, but a good implementation consultant can make success sure, less painful, and occur more quickly. The last point is perhaps the most crucial. With so many companies pursuing similar product development improvement goals, the key to superiority lies in how fast the changes can be fully implemented. The experienced outsider can bring knowledge from implementing change within similar companies, which is invaluable if the company is to avoid making the same time-costly mistakes others have already made. He or she can bring a clearer vision of what must be accomplished first and, based on actual experience, what may be deferred. He or she can bring objectivity and a distance from internal, political issues. In particular, the experienced PACE implementor will be more likely to succeed in those activities focused on senior management than a member of that management's organization.

Executive Leadership

A company's CEO and other members of executive management have the primary responsibility for improving a company's core business processes, and none is more critical today than product development. Driving the improvement of new product development is often the most important contribution that the CEO can make to the long-term success of the company. New products drive the growth and prosperity of most companies. Yet a CEO or the executive management team can't lead every product development activity — there isn't enough time. The CEO and the executive team can, however, lead the creation of the best possible process for developing new products.

They can initiate the change process. This entails setting new objectives for product development, establishing a new direction for the process of developing products, and launching the project to change that process. This provides the vision necessary for everyone in the company to make these very difficult changes.

Finally, they can help maintain the course. This is most essential when the change process is at a difficult juncture. When the new product development process is partially, but not yet fully, implemented the benefits are not yet apparent — but the stress of the change on individuals is. Some see their responsibilities changing and are uncertain what this will mean to them, so they

cross-functional   The involvement of multiple functions working on common development *steps*, in an integrated manner, at the same time instead of sequentially.

cross-project management   The management of those activities, such as *resource scheduling* and *portfolio management*, that affect multiple projects. This is also an element of the *PACE* process.

cycle time   The time required to complete a particular process or *step* within a process, such as the *product development process*.

cycle-time guidelines   Within *PACE*, a characterization of a company's *product development process* at the *step* level from a time perspective that is used for scheduling and continuous improvement; a standard costing for time.

defining technology   The technology that principally defines the performance or cost advantage of a product or *product platform*; usually a *core technology*.

design for excellence (DFE)   Design approaches that incorporate more than performance or features into product design. Includes such techniques as design for manufacturability/assembly, design for logistics, design for testability, design for serviceability, and design for green (environmental considerations).

design techniques   Practices used in new product development to design products better and faster. Each technique has a specific focus.

detailed development guidelines   A set of procedures and visual aids for accomplishing development *steps*. These are the "how to" of the process.

empowerment   The act of giving a group, typically a project team, the responsibility and authority to do a specific job. Should not be confused with letting them do anything they want without an approval process.

engineering change orders (ECOs)   The documentation and process for changing products once they are released.

full project team   The full team involved in development, including the *Core Team* and the *support team* (those outside of the Core Team, many of whom are not dedicated to one project).

future core technologies   The *core technologies* of the future, with the potential to alter the rules of competition; sometimes called pacing technologies.

PACE® (Product And Cycle-time Excellence®)   A term introduced by *PRTM* that defines both a philosophy (achieving excellence in the quality and market success of new products while simultaneously achieving the shortest *time-to-market*) and an approach to implementing the philosophy; a framework that integrates the elements of the *product development process*.

PACE engineer   The *PACE* process owner after implementation; responsible for continuous improvement and *product development process* engineering; sometimes called PACE manager.

phase   A major stage of product development within a *Phase Review Process*. Each phase has specific requirements that projects must fulfill to continue into the next phase.

phase review The milestone at the end of a *phase* in a *Phase Review Process* where approval is required in order to proceed. Usually this requires resolving specific issues.

Phase Review Process The process within *PACE* where senior management (as a *PAC*) approves new product development, allocates development resources, and prioritizes activities. Within PACE, this is an action-oriented process that implements *product strategy* and initiates empowerment of *Core Teams*. It does so through a series of focused and efficient presentations.

pipeline loading An element of *pipeline management*; it fine-tunes the aggregate project schedule to actively manage the entry and exit of development projects into the pipeline and *Phase Review Process* and seamlessly handles mid-course corrections.

pipeline loading profile A graphical tool used to monitor and maintain pipeline balance; during *strategic balancing*, this profile is used to create an aggregate project schedule that is in balance with the company's resource and skill capacity.

pipeline management One of the seven interrelated elements of *PACE*. This element optimizes deployment of resources by aligning *product strategy* with project and functional management.

portfolio management The process for managing the types of projects in order to achieve a strategic mix of technologies, timeframe, risk, markets, and business segments.

Product Approval Committee (PAC) The senior management group that has the authority and responsibility to approve and prioritize new product development within a *Phase Review Process*. Sometimes called by other terms, such as project approval committee, product review board, executive committee, strategy committee.

product development process The overall business process for developing new products. While frequently referred to, there is no generally accepted description of how it actually works.

product development process engineering The responsibility for planning and continuous improvement of the *product development process* itself. A responsibility of the *PACE engineer*.

product line A grouping of products released over time from a common *product platform*.

product line expansion The element of *product strategy* that focuses on expanding current *product lines*.

product line plan A time-phased conditional plan for the sequence of developing products within a *product line*.

product platform The collection of common technical elements, especially the underlying *core technology*, implemented across a range of products. It is primarily a definition for planning, development, and strategic decision making.

product positioning A *product strategy* technique for defining products to have strategically favorable advantages in the market relative to competitors.

Index